Great Walks of the Olympic Peninsula

Text by Robert Gillmore

Photographs by Eileen Oktavec

D0324602

To Vern Winslow Gillmore and
Helen Marion Tyre Gillmore,
with much love.

Great Walks®

No. 7 in a series of full-color, pocket-size guides to the best walks in the world published by Great Walks Inc. Other Great Walks guides: *Great Walks of Acadia National Park & Mount Desert Island*, *Great Walks of Southern Arizona*, *Great Walks of Big Bend National Park*, *Great Walks of the Great Smokies*, *Great Walks of Yosemite National Park*, and *Great Walks of Sequoia & Kings Canyon National Parks*. For more information on all Great Walks guides send $1 (refundable with your first order) to: Great Walks, PO Box 410, Goffstown, NH 03045.

*COVER: The **Wolf Creek Trail** (Walk No. 3) provides continuous views of the glacier-covered 6,995-foot massif of Mt. Carrie.*

CONTENTS

PACIFIC COAST

RAIN FORESTS

HOOD CANAL REGION

What Are Great Walks?

Great Walks are usually shorter and easier than the typical hike or climb. They're usually less than five miles long. They can be walked in a day or less. And they're usually on smooth, firm, dry, and *gently graded* trails.

Most important, Great Walks invariably offer beautiful and interesting world-class scenery and excellent, often continuous views in the most celebrated natural areas on earth.

What Are Great Walks Guides?

Great Walks guides carefully describe and, with beautiful full-color photographs, lavishly illustrate the world's Great Walks.

Unlike many walking guides, which describe *every* trail in a region, Great Walks describe only the *best* walks, the happy few that will especially delight you with their beauty.

Unlike many guides, which give you mainly directions, Great Walks guides carefully describe *all* the major features of every Great Walk, so you can know, in advance, *precisely* what the Walk has to offer and exactly *why* it's worth your time to take it.

After all, your leisure time is valuable. In your lifetime you can walk on only a fraction of the hundreds of thousands of miles of trails in the world. Why not walk only the best?

For your convenience Great Walks guides are an easy-to-use and easy-to-carry pocket size and their covers are film-laminated for extra protection against wear and tear.

Acknowledgments

We are grateful for the assistance of Bill Baccus, Janis Burger, Paul Crawford, Matt Graves, Roger Hoffman, Dan Johnson, Francis Kocis, Barb Maynes, John Meyer, Susan Schultz, Chiggers Stokes, and John Wullschleger of the National Park Service; Kate Snow of the US Forest Service; and Alice Langebartel of the Makah tribe.

Foreword: The Many Splendors of the Olympics — and How to Enjoy Them

Some places are celebrated for their seacoasts, some for their mountains, others for their forests, lakes, or rivers. Washington's Olympic Peninsula—the northwesternmost point of the continental United States—is distinguished not for just one of these things but for splendid examples of them all: wild Pacific beaches; temperate rain forests dominated by giant evergreens; wildflower-dappled subalpine meadows; glacier-covered peaks; thrilling cascading rivers; dazzling waterfalls; and stunning mountain-rimmed lakes. The Olympic Peninsula has an amazing diversity of amazing scenery.

You can savor all this beauty on the peninsula's 62 Great Walks and three Honorable Mentions.

The region has more Great Walks than any other area of its size in America. Olympic National Park alone has 42. Nearly all the other walks are in the Olympic National Forest, which surrounds most of the park. Two are on Indian reservations adjacent to the park and one—Rocky Brook Falls—is on private land close to the national forest.

Eight Great Walks—Nos. 2-9—are in mile-high subalpine meadows where you stroll among blooming wildflowers and enjoy views usually reserved for mountain climbers: glorious, uninterrupted panoramas of snowcapped Olympic peaks.

Fourteen Walks—Nos. 22-32 and 34-36—and Honorable Mention No. 3 are along unspoiled Pacific beaches, where you see spruce-covered off-shore islands; jagged sea stacks, caves, cliffs, arches, and other dramatic rock formations; starfish, anemones, and other curious sea life; and fascinating Indian petroglyphs.

Walk No. 21 takes you to monumental headlands at the northwesternmost tip of the continental United States.

Nine Walks—Nos. 37-45—run through lush temperate rain forests soaked by as much as 200 inches of rain per year—moist, mossy jungles where Sitka spruces and other evergreen trees grow more than 12 feet thick.

Seven Walks—Nos. 11, 12, 15, 19, 46, 52, and 56—take you to impressive waterfalls.

Eleven Walks—Nos. 10, 13, 17, 19, 43, 44, 47, 48, 53, 55, and 60—offer exciting vistas of cascading streams.

Three Walks—Nos. 5, 16 and 58—and Honorable Mention No. 2 provide views of mountain-rimmed lakes.

Honorable Mention No. 1 brings you to a half dozen small pools fed by natural hot springs.

Sixteen Walks—Nos. 2, 8, 14, 18, 20, 33, 38, 39, 41, 43, 45, 50, 51, 54, 57, and 60—are mostly easy or undemanding "nature trails" where interesting signs or illustrated pamphlets describe the phenomena seen en route.

Some or all of the route of 15 Walks—Nos. 1, 2, 4, 11, 14, 17, 20, 38-40, 46, 49-51, and 54—are wheelchair accessible. These paths, which include many of the nature trails listed above, have paved or smooth gravel surfaces, and they're either level or very gently graded.

Ocean Walks

Paradoxically, beaches can be both the smoothest walks on the Olympic Peninsula or the roughest. This is why: A typical Olympic beach usually consists of at least three parallel zones: (1) heaps of rocks stretching along the highest part of the beach, or driftwood washed up by fierce winter storms; (2) a band of much smaller rocks below the big piles of rocks or logs; and (3) a strip of sand near the water. The sand, usually moist, is one of the best walking surfaces anywhere—smooth and just firm enough for effortless strolling. The rocks above the sand, on the other hand, are one of the worst, and the piles of rocks and driftwood above those are all but impassable.

The problem, of course, is that the sand is the first thing to disappear in a rising tide. In other words, the unhappy first law of Olympic beach walking is: The best footing is the one most likely to be under water. On some beaches the strip of sand is narrow, and the narrower it is—this is the second law of Olympic beach walking—the more quickly it's covered by a rising tide.

So the most important thing to remember about beach walks—call it the third law of Olympic beach walking—is: *To maximize your chances of walking on sand, not rocks, take these walks at the lowest possible tide.*

Tide tables are available at many places on the

Olympic Peninsula, including ranger stations, stores, resorts, and other accommodations; they're also posted at most beach trailheads and published in many local newspapers and telephone directories.

Several Walks, including Cape Alava (No. 22), Rialto Beach (No. 24), and Ruby Beach (No. 29), are relatively long excursions because they include double round trips: You follow the beach for some distance in one direction, then return to the starting point; then you walk the beach in the other direction before coming back again to the starting point. Sometimes the tide may get too high before you finish. You may want to divide these Walks into two trips, walking the beach in one direction on one day, the other direction on another day.

If you must walk a beach at high or medium tide, try one with a relatively wide strip of sand, such as Beach 1 or 2 (Walks No. 36 and 35) near Kalaloch Lodge. Or pick a beach that's close to the trailhead; that way, if you find that the tide is too high when you get there, you won't have lost much time walking to or from it. Beaches near trailheads include Rialto and First Beach at LaPush (Walks No. 24 and 25) and every beach on the Kalaloch Coast (Walks No. 28-36).

If you don't have enough low tides (or time) to take all 15 beach walks, here's some information to help you narrow your choices:

▶ The best collections of sea stacks and other natural ocean sculpture are at Ruby Beach (Walk No. 29), on the Kalaloch Coast, and every beach at or near LaPush (Walks No. 24-27).

▶ You'll see starfish (also known as sea stars), sea

anemones, and other sea life at Ruby Beach, Beach 3, and Beach 4 (Walks No. 29, 32, and 31 respectively) on the Kalaloch Coast and on all the LaPush area beaches (Walks No. 24-27).

▶ Beaches with dramatic ocean overlooks close to the parking areas are Oil City, Ruby, Kalaloch, Beach 1, Beach 3, Beach 4, and Beach 6 (Walks No. 28, 29, 34, 36, 32, 31, and 30 respectively), all on the Kalaloch Coast.

Unfortunately, these beaches are not great for swimming. The water is rarely warmer than 55 degrees Fahrenheit—too cold for most people—currents are often strong, and large floating logs can cause serious injuries and even death.

* * *

None of these walks is very strenuous. In fact, 20 of them, or about one third of the total—Nos. 1, 3, 11, 14, 17, 18, 20, 25, 33-35, 37, 41, 45, 46, 49-52, and 54—are either easy or very easy, and 20 others—Nos. 2, 6, 8, 9, 21, 26, 28, 30-32, 36, 38-39, 43, 48, 57, 59-61, and Honorable Mention No. 2—while not exactly easy, are nevertheless undemanding; 21 walks—Nos. 4, 7, 10, 12, 13, 15, 19, 22-24, 27, 40, 42, 44, 47, 53, 55, 56, 62, and Honorable Mentions No. 1 and 3—are moderate. Only three Walks—Nos. 5, 16, and 58—are moderately strenuous. One Walk—No. 29—can be either easy or moderate depending on how much of Ruby Beach you want to explore.

Most of the walks are on smooth, firm, dry paths, and most of the trails are either level or gently graded. The few exceptions to this rule are noted.

Most walks are short: 22 are a mile or less; 43 are three miles or less. Only 11 are five miles or more.

The longest, No. 22, is 9.6 miles.

How much time do the walks take? That depends, of course, on how fast you walk. But a rough rule of thumb is: one hour per mile. If you walk faster and don't pause to enjoy the views (see below), the time, of course, is less.

The average walk takes just a few hours, the shortest ones just a few minutes, the longest one (No. 22) no more than eight or nine hours.

Depending on your speed, and on how much walking you want to do each day, it takes about 26 to 35 days to do every walk in the book.

The very best Walks—those with the most exciting ocean, river, rain forest, or mountain scenery—are those on or near Hurricane Ridge (Nos. 2-7) and Nos. 8, 11, 15, 19, 21, 24, 29, 38, and 60.

What's the best time to take these walks? Whenever it's least likely to rain; on the Olympic Peninsula, that's the summer. The Northwest is one of the wettest places in the world, but, conveniently for vacationers, most of the rain and snow falls between October and May. Summers are relatively dry. We've walked the Olympics from June to late September, and it seldom rained any more then than it does in New England.

Summer has other advantages, too. The snow is gone from virtually every trail, and the weather is often ideal for walking: neither too cool nor too warm. The temperature rarely falls below 50, even at night, and 80 is considered hot. Of course, the earlier in the summer you visit waterfalls and cascading streams, the fuller and more exciting they'll be. (Most of the waterfalls in this guide were described in the summer. They may look different in wetter or drier weather.)

Remember, however, that the peninsula's weather is not guaranteed. It *can* be rainy and cold (especially at upper elevations) even in August. So it's wise to be prepared for it with rain gear and warm clothes (see below).

Here are some more tips to help you get the most out of these walks:

▶ This guide tells you exactly what each walk has to offer. Take advantage of it by reading it before you take any walks. That way you'll be best able to select trails most closely suited to your taste.

▶ Carry this guide on every walk. (It'll fit easily in your pocket or pack.) Besides detailed descriptions of what you'll see, it also tells you how to reach the trailhead and gives you precise directions for each trail.

▶ The walks start where they start, stop where they stop, and go where they go for two reasons: (1) the routes we describe are the best walks in the area; (2) any other routes are more difficult, less scenic, or both. The Olympic Peninsula has hundreds of miles of trails, but only the routes described below are Great Walks or Honorable Mentions.

▶ The walks we describe can be taken without maps. Most trails are easy to follow, and in any event we tell you everything you need to know to find your way. We also point out every natural landmark you'll see.

The Park Service does recommend, however, that hikers carry maps as a safety precaution, and a detailed, easy-to-read topographic map may help you identify natural landmarks. The best topographic map of the entire Olympic National Park—the one that indicates the largest number of features in the clearest way—is the 1:100,000-scale map *Olympic National Park and Vicinity* published by the US Geological Survey. The best topographic maps of particular sections of the park and other areas of the Olympic Peninsula are published by Custom Correct. They're all available at ranger stations, visitor centers, and stores.

Also helpful for getting around the area is the park's free *Official Map and Guide*. Like all similar National Park Service publications, it clearly and attractively indicates all roads in and near the park as well as trails and other natural and manmade features. Pick it up at any visitor center, entrance station, or ranger station.

The Park Service has also published free sketch maps of the roads and trails on Hurricane Ridge (pages 20-69), in the Elwha Valley (pages 84-95), at the Olympic Hot Springs (pages 314-320), around Lake Crescent (pages 96-111), in the Sol Duc Valley (pages 118-132), and along the Pacific Coast (pages 144-212). These maps, which cover almost all the Great Walks and Honorable Mentions in the park, are available at ranger stations and the visitor center in Port Angeles.

The Olympic National Forest has produced a simple map of roads and trailheads in the Hood Canal region (pages 252-313); it's available free at the Quilcene and Hoodsport ranger stations. The Forest Service has also printed an attractive map of the Lake Quinault area (pages 226-251) and a separate map of the trails just south of the lake (Walks No. 43 and 44); both are available without charge at the Quinault Ranger Station. The Forest Service website (www.olympus.net/onf) publishes the latest trail conditions.

▶ Along with directions to each trailhead, we also describe interesting features you'll see along the way, as well as campgrounds and accommodations near the trailheads. We also list local chambers of commerce, which can provide more information on services in the area. More than 200 places to stay are listed in the pamphlet *Lodging on the Olympic Peninsula,* available free from the Peninsula Tourism Coalition, PO Box F, Carlsborg, WA 98324.

▶ To help you identify wildflowers and other flora, the park maintains excellent collections of specimens, encased in clear plastic, at the Port Angeles, Hurricane Ridge, and Hoh Rain Forest visitor centers.

▶ Unless you're in excellent condition (and few people are) do your body a favor: Whenever possible, do the easiest walks first. That way each walk will help prepare you to take a harder one. Ideally, you'll progress from short, easy walks to longer, more difficult ones with no difficulty.

▶ Try to do walks with long-range views—the Hurricane Ridge area trails, for instance—on bright, sunny days, when the vistas will be clearest. Save walks with short-range views—rain-forest trails, waterfalls, and other in-the-woods paths—for cloudy days.

▶ Snow lingers on upper-elevation trails—such as those on Hurricane Ridge—until early summer and sometimes even later. Be sure the path is clear before heading out.

▶ Any comfortable walking shoes are fine for short walks that follow smooth paths. For walks on longer, less-beaten trails we recommend the greater support and protection of above-the-ankle hiking boots. To avoid unnecessary discomfort (including blisters) make sure your footwear fits and is broken in before you start walking. Waterproofed boots are nice to have on stream crossings, beach walks, and rain-forest walks, and they're especially welcome on rainy days.

▶ Carry rain gear. For best protection, we recommend a lightweight waterproof jacket and pants. The most comfortable rain garments are made of "breathable" Goretex fabric, which keeps rain out but also lets perspiration escape.

▶ Carry water on longer walks. It will taste best if you carry it in ceramic canteens, such as the French-made Tournus, rather than plastic or metal bottles. If you have access to a refrigerator, here's a way to keep the water cold: The night before a walk pour just an inch or so of water in the canteen and lay it on its side in the freezer, leaving the top open to make sure the canteen doesn't crack when the water freezes and expands. Next morning fill the canteen with cold water. The ice already inside will keep the water cold.

▶ Never drink water from any stream or spring without boiling it or treating it with purifying tablets. The risk of an attack of *giardia lamblia* is too great to drink untreated water.

▶ Never urinate or defecate within 100 feet of

streams or lakes and don't wash up in them. Even biodegradable soap pollutes lakes and streams if used directly in them.

▶ Subalpine meadows are fragile. To avoid disturbing them, stay on established paths.

▶ It's obvious but it bears repeating: Binoculars enable you to see what you can't see or see as well without them (bald eagles, for example). A high-powered, lightweight pair is worth carrying.

▶ Use enough sunscreen to protect the exposed parts of your body, and wear something to keep the sun out of your eyes, especially when walking on beaches, in meadows, and other places where you're constantly in the open.

▶ Mosquitoes and other flying insects can be a pesty problem, especially in warmer weather. Consider carrying some repellent, just in case.

▶ Many viewpoints are unfenced overlooks on the edge of sheer bluffs. A fall from them would ruin your vacation, if not your life; so use caution and keep hold of children's hands.

▶ Be sure to begin each walk early enough so you can finish it comfortably before dark.

▶ On longer walks, carry a small flashlight in case you can't get back before dark, as well as some toilet paper and Band-Aids. Both the Park Service and the Forest Service also recommend what they call the "ten essentials." These include not only sunglasses, flashlight, and a map, but also a knife, a compass, matches, a first aid kit, and extra clothing, food and water.

▶ Cars parked at trailheads are occasionally vandalized. As precautions, lock your vehicle and don't leave valuables in it; if you must leave them, lock them in the trunk.

▶ Trail passes are required to park at national forest trailheads. They can be bought at ranger stations and many stores in or near the Olympic National Forest. The cost is $3 per vehicle per day or $25 a year.

▶ Remember that the world's only constant is change. The locations of the lakes and mountains on these walks won't vary from year to year, but anything subject to human control—trail routes, parking lots, signs, and so on—can change. Be alert for trail reroutings and follow signs.

▶ Above all, remember that a Great Walk is mainly an aesthetic, not an athletic activity. Its primary purpose is not to give you exercise (although exercise you will surely get) but to expose you to exceptional natural beauty. Walk slowly enough to savor it. Some people walk too fast. Don't make their mistake. You no more want to rush through these walks than you want to rush through the Louvre.

NORTH PENINSULA

Great Walks No. 1-20 and Honorable Mentions No. 1 and 2 are all in the northern part of the Olympic Peninsula.

Hurricane Ridge Area

Walks No. 1-7 all begin on the Hurricane Ridge or Obstruction Point roads—two of the highest and most scenic routes in the Olympics—in the north-central region of Olympic National Park.

Walks No. 2-7 are the most spectacular Great Walks on the peninsula because they're all above timberline. Without trees in the way they offer uninterrupted views of snow-capped Olympic peaks and subalpine meadows.

Accommodations in the area include the park's Heart O' the Hills Campground and about 30 restaurants and almost two dozen motels and B&Bs in **Port Angeles,** the largest city on the Olympic Peninsula. The Port Angeles Chamber of Commerce (121 East Railroad St., Port Angeles, WA 98362; 360-452-2363) publishes free directories of local services.

* * *

Hurricane Ridge Road, the third highest on the Olympic Peninsula, begins at the national park entrance, at the southern end of Race Street in Port Angeles.

The road immediately passes the **visitor center,** on your right, which has rest rooms, interesting exhibits, a large selection of books and other publications, and rangers and volunteers on hand to answer questions.

The paved road then climbs gently through a mixed evergreen and deciduous forest. You'll have occasional views of Klahhane Ridge (Walk No. 5) and 6,454-foot Mt. Angeles, at the western end of the ridge, rising straight ahead of you.

About 4.5 miles from the visitor center you'll come to an overlook, on the left, from which you can see across the Strait of Juan de Fuca to the San Juan Islands and the Cascade Mountains. On a clear day you'll see snow-covered 10,778-foot Mt. Baker, the highest peak on the horizon. Off to your right are several Olympic summits, including 6,007-foot Blue Mountain (Walks No. 8 and 9) and 3,591-foot Round Mountain.

In another .9 miles you'll be at the park entrance station. **Heart O' the Hills Campground** is just ahead, on the left.

Then the road climbs gracefully through a forest of mature Douglas firs and hemlocks until, about 3.8 miles beyond the entrance station, it reaches **Lookout Rock** *(Walk No. 1),* on the left. The view from the parking area is described on page 29.

Immediately after Lookout Rock the road passes

through three tunnels cut into the basalt flanks of 4,910-foot Burnt Mountain, which forms the eastern shoulder of Klahhane Ridge.

Then the road curves around to the south side of Klahhane Ridge. The lower slope of the ridge plunges into Morse Creek Canyon, on your left, and the pointed mile-high summits of the eastern end of Hurricane Ridge, snow-capped even in summer, sweep up the south side of the valley.

You've now climbed more than 3,000 feet above sea level. Here, on the sunny, drier south slope of Klahhane Ridge, Douglas firs and hemlocks thin out. Instead of the thick, lush forest you drove through on the wetter north side of the ridge, you now pass lots of bare ground and, later, the beginnings of sub-alpine meadows dotted with clusters of subalpine firs.

About 2.8 miles beyond Lookout Rock you come to another overlook, on the left, with a sweeping view across Morse Creek Valley. The vista, from   left to right, includes Round Mountain, Blue Mountain— note the Deer Park Road (pages 70-73) going across it—and the eastern end of Hurricane Ridge. On a clear day you can see 10,541-foot Glacier Peak, in the Cascades, between Round and Blue mountains.

In another 3.2 miles you'll pass the bottom of the Switchback Trail (page 54), on the right. About 1.8 miles beyond it, look up and you'll see steep sub-alpine meadows decorated with thick clusters of sub-alpine fir. On the horizon, on the left, is Alpine Hill;

◄ *Mist and clouds rise from Morse Creek Valley, east of the* **Hurricane Ridge Road.**

on the right is Sunrise Point; both summits and the long ridge between them are on the Hurricane Ridge Nature Trails (Walk No. 2). Running across the meadow is the Klahhane Ridge Trail (Walk No. 5).

In another .5 miles you'll see Steeple Rock, a handsome stone finial on top of the eastern arm of Hurricane Ridge. To the right of the ridge you'll see snowcapped peaks of the inner Olympics.

About .5 miles farther the **Obstruction Point Road** (see below) comes in on the left.

About .2 miles past the junction is the **Hurricane Ridge Visitor Center. Walk No. 2** (the **Hurricane Ridge Nature Trails**) and **Walk No. 5** (**Klahhane Ridge**) begin on the north side of the parking area.

The handsome, sturdy visitor center is a very agreeable place. Finished with warm wooden paneling, the first floor has bathrooms, comfortable couches, a fireplace, huge windows with an expansive view into the heart of the Olympics, and excellent exhibits on the geology, history, trees, flowers, and animals of the region. There's also a large three-dimensional model of the park, which depicts it better than any map.

The basement contains more rest rooms, a gift shop, and a small but well-stocked snack bar serving hot and cold sandwiches, soups, and a variety of drinks, sweets, and other treats.

Along the front of the building is a delightful patio framed by a low stone wall and furnished with wooden picnic tables. The terrace has what some say is the best view in the Olympics. Directly below it a vast subalpine meadow descends to the Lillian and

Elwha river valleys; Columbia black-tailed deer graze in the grass. Rising thousands of feet up from the valleys is a broad semicircle of literally dozens of snowcapped Olympic peaks, including 7,965-foot Mt. Olympus, tallest of them all; a plaque at the wall identifies the summits. The setting reminds us of Switzerland; it's a superlative spot for a leisurely picnic.

After passing the visitor center, the road gets narrower and runs along the crest of Hurricane Ridge.

About .7 miles after the visitor center you'll come to the **Wolf Creek Trail** *(Walk No. 3)*. At the trailhead and at several places along the road before it, you'll have views to the north that sweep from Hurricane Hill (Walk No. 4) on the left, to the Strait of Juan de Fuca, to the massif of Mt. Angeles on the right. (See page 39 for a detailed description.)

In another .3 miles you'll come to Picnic Area A, on the left, which has wonderful mountain views to the south. About .1 miles beyond it is Picnic Area B, also on the left.

Finally, .3 miles beyond the second picnic area and 19.6 miles from the park entrance, the road ends at a parking loop by the **Hurricane Hill Trail** *(Walk No. 4)*.

* * *

Walk No. 6, the **Obstruction Point-Deer Park Trail,** and **Walk No. 7, Lillian Ridge**, begin at the end of the mile-high **Obstruction Point Road**, the highest road on the Olympic Peninsula. Running on or near the crest of the eastern arm of Hurricane Ridge, the road offers spectacular vistas both north and south, including the best views of Mt. Olympus from

any highway. The route, however, is unpaved, narrow, and sometimes very close to the edge of a steep meadow, on the right, that plunges hundreds of feet down to Lillian Creek; so drive carefully.

The road begins on the Hurricane Ridge Road, about .2 miles east of the Hurricane Ridge Visitor Center (page 24). At first it traverses a steep meadow on the south side of the ridge. Lillian Creek Valley drops off to the right. In the distance are the snowcapped Olympics.

The road descends to a saddle on the ridge, passes through a patch of evergreen woods, and, about 1.5 miles from the Hurricane Ridge Road, emerges into a clearing where you have a brief view of Klahhane Ridge, on the left. Just ahead of you is the pointed Steeple Rock, on the crest of the ridge.

The road runs along the south side of the ridge, past Steeple Rock, and again you have a wide view of the Olympics. As you go farther along the road, Mt. Olympus will become more and more prominent and its appearance ever more distinctive. Most of the other mountains are more blue than white because they have relatively little snow on their flanks, or none at all. Olympus is different. It's almost all white because it's covered by vast glaciers

◀ *Cow parsnips bloom in July along the **Obstruction Point Road**, which has the best views of Mt. Olympus from any road on the Olympic Peninsula. Olympus' glacier-covered summits are the highest peaks on the horizon; summits of the Bailey Range are in front of and to the right of the 7,965-foot massif. In front of the mountains, long, steep ridges separate the (from rear to front) Long Creek, Elwha River, and Lillian River valleys.*

draped over the broad slopes that connect its several summits.

After about 2.8 miles the road goes back into the woods. But about 1.6 miles later it comes out into the open again and switches back and forth up toward the crest of the ridge. Now you'll see not only snowy peaks to the south and west but also Hurricane Hill (Walk No. 4), Mt. Angeles, and other landmarks near the Hurricane Ridge Visitor Center.

After about six miles you'll see smooth meadows on 6,450-foot Obstruction Peak, the second highest point on Hurricane Ridge; snowfields linger on the flanks of the peak into late summer.

In another .2 miles you'll be back on a broad saddle on the crest of the ridge. From the turnout on the left you'll have a view down Morse Creek Valley and as far north as the Strait of Juan de Fuca.

Now the road traverses the sweeping treeless meadows along the south side of the ridge and, about 7.8 miles from the Hurricane Ridge Road, ends in a parking area on the south flank of Obstruction Peak. Walks No. 6 and 7 begin at the signboards at the end of the road.

1 Lookout Rock

This very easy .1-mile round trip—the shortest Great Walk in the Olympics—takes you through a delightful gardenlike evergreen woods to a dramatic view of Morse Creek Valley.

The Walk begins at an overlook on the east side of Hurricane Ridge Road, about 9.2 miles past the park visitor center. From the overlook you can see the Strait of Juan de Fuca, more than 2,400 feet below. On a clear day you can also see (from left to right) the Canadian city of Victoria, on Vancouver Island in British Columbia, on the far side of the strait; the San Juan Islands to the northeast; and, farther east, the snowcapped Cascade Mountains; look for the white dome of 10,778-foot Mt. Baker, Washington's fourth-highest peak. On the south shore of the strait you can see the long, flat, skinny Dungeness Spit. Reaching six miles into the strait, it's the country's longest natural sand spit. The white lighthouse near the end was built in 1857.

A sign here notes that the Sequim Prairie, just south of the spit, gets only 20 inches of rain a year (which makes it easily the driest place on the Olympic Peninsula), while, ironically, the rain forest just 50 miles to the west gets 140 to 180 inches a year. The reason is that the Olympic Mountains, which lie between the rain forest and the prairie, absorb most of the precipitation that would otherwise fall on Sequim.

From the southern end of the overlook, a four-foot-wide asphalt path curves gently through an evergreen woods, around handsome low basalt rocks and past pleasing, solid sweeps of moss, low salal, bearberry, and twinflower. The setting is so neat it looks like a woodland garden.

The path ends at Lookout Rock, an impressive round concrete overlook with a stunning vista. The steep forested slopes of Morse Creek Valley plunge

hundreds of feet down to the creek. On the left, the 3,541-foot summit of Round Mountain soars almost 2,000 feet above the floor of the valley. On the right are the massive rounded, buttresslike cliffs of 4,910-foot Burnt Mountain, festooned with evergreens. In the center of the vista is the eastern end of Hurricane Ridge (Walk No. 6), whose precipitous 6,000-plus-foot slopes are snow-flecked even in late summer. Listen carefully and you may hear the shooshing of Morse Creek, 1,000 feet below.

After you've enjoyed the view, retrace your steps to your car.

2 Hurricane Ridge Nature Trails

This undemanding two-mile loop may be the greatest Walk in the Olympics. As you stroll along mile-high ridge-top paths, you'll enjoy dramatic, nearly continuous views of a plunging glacial cirque; major mountain peaks; steep river-carved mountain valleys; the northern Olympic coast; the Strait of Juan de Fuca; and, on a clear day, British Columbia. In the

◄ *The Hurricane Ridge Road provides dramatic views of Hurricane Ridge, whose summits are studded with snow even in summer. Exuberant drifts of lavender lupine festoon the roadside.*

summer the subalpine meadows along the trails are bright with wildflowers. The vistas, the flowers, and the natural history of the ridge are all described and illustrated by more than a dozen well-written trailside signs.

The Walk begins at the 5,242-foot-high Hurricane Ridge Visitor Center, which is about 18 miles from Port Angeles on the Hurricane Ridge Road. (See pages 20-25 for a description of what you'll see along the way.) The trail begins about 200 feet west of the visitor center, on the opposite side of the road.

Since much of the Walk follows the first part of Walk No. 5 (Klahhane Ridge), both Walks can be combined into one (admittedly long) excursion. See pages 47-48.

This Walk first follows the paved Cirque Rim Trail, which gently climbs up to the crest of Hurricane Ridge. On both sides of the trail are thick clusters of subalpine fir trees. As signs on the Walk explain, their tall, narrow shape—which resembles the spires of a Gaudí cathedral—allows the trees to shed snow easily; by growing in dense clusters they protect each other from snow, sleet, and fierce winter winds. As other signs point out, these subalpine meadows are blanketed by as much as ten feet of snow in the winter, and even on relatively warm, south-facing slopes, some of the snow doesn't melt until August. Thistles, avalanche lilies, glacier lilies, lavender subalpine lupine, and other wildflowers bloom here in the summer—sometimes beside patches of snow. Avalanche lilies will even come up *through* snow! Turn around and you'll see snow that never melts—

the glaciers on top of Mt. Carrie and Mt. Olympus.

Less than .1 miles from the road you'll come to the narrow crest of Hurricane Ridge. At this point the crest is also the south rim of a vast cirque, a glacier-carved amphitheater whose steep, semicircular sides plunge hundreds of feet down the valley of the South Branch of the Little River. These north-facing slopes get much less sun than the south-facing ones behind you, so at least a few patches of snow linger here as late as September.

The 180-degree view from the rim is one of the Walk's most dramatic. On your far left is 5,757-foot Hurricane Hill (Walk No. 4). To the right of Hurricane Hill is the rocky knob of 5,100-foot Unicorn Peak. Unicorn Horn is to the right of Unicorn Peak, and 5,113-foot Griff Peak is to the right of Unicorn Horn. Directly below you is the mile-deep valley of the South Branch. In the distance is the Olympic coast and the Strait of Juan de Fuca. Fifteen miles across the strait is Vancouver Island; on a clear day you'll see the buildings of Victoria. The San Juan Islands are to the northeast. To your right, less than .4 miles away, is Sunrise Point, where you'll see another great view in a few minutes. To the right of the point is Sunrise Ridge. Behind the ridge is the rocky top of 6,454-foot Mount Angeles. To the right of the ridge is 5,471-foot Alpine Hill, which has a sweeping view as well.

After you've savored the vista, take the 250-foot spur trail that follows the narrow crest of the ridge to your left. As you walk down to the viewpoint at the end of the ridge, the slope drops sharply on your right and your wide vista to the north continues;

you'll also be able to see back toward the precipitous walls of the cirque. The first time I saw this south view, I thought: Here the world is all steepness, consisting only of plunging grassy meadows punctuated by the green spires of subalpine firs. The only thing level in this giddy world is the thin, narrow crest running along the very top of it.

Follow the spur trail back to the Cirque Rim Trail, which, true to its name, curves along the top of the bowl. Look behind you and you'll see landmarks on the ridge to the west of the Elwha River Valley— 6,000-foot Mt. Appleton and 5,600-foot Boulder Peak.

About .1 miles from the spur trail you'll come to an intersection. Go straight ahead, along the rim, and enjoy the uninterrupted views. In another .2 miles or so you'll see a ski lift on the slope of the cirque to your left and a ski patrol building on your right. Like the subalpine firs, the steep-sided A-frame structure is built to shed snow.

The climate is so harsh here that the fir trees grow at, well, glacial speed. A tree only two or three feet high could actually be 50 to 80 years old. A clever sign nearby notes that many of the firs are so small that they spend the majority of their lives under snow!

Almost immediately after the ski lift, you'll come to another intersection. Take a left onto the unpaved High Ridge Trail. (From here to the four-way junction at the top of Sunrise Ridge, the route will be the same as the beginning of Walk No. 5 [Klahhane Ridge].) The path switches back and forth through a shady grove of subalpine firs as it makes a short but sometimes steep climb up Sunrise Ridge. Make the climb easier by pausing often to enjoy the view through the trees on your left: Hurricane Hill (notice the trail across the meadow), Unicorn Peak, Unicorn Horn, Griff Peak, and especially the vast gaping cirque at the head of the South Branch of the Little River.

As the trail approaches the top of Sunrise Ridge it reemerges into open meadows, and you have sweeping views to the south and west. The trail passes through lupine, magenta paintbrush, and pink heather, all blooming in midsummer, and reaches a four-way junction in a saddle, or low point, in the long, narrow Sunrise Ridge. You're now on a knife edge between two valleys—the Little River on your left, Cox on the right—that plunge sharply on each side. Elegant clusters of pointed subalpine firs spread over the smooth green slopes of the steep meadows.

The view on the ridge is panoramic. To the southwest, beyond the Bailey Range, is glacier-capped Mt. Olympus, framed dramatically by subalpine firs. To the west is the cirque and the summits beyond it. To the north are the steep, treeless slopes of a spur ridge, its east side almost surrealistically flat and its knife-edge crest just wide enough for a trail. The little peak on the ridge, .1 miles away, is Sunrise Point. West of Sunrise Point, an arm of the ridge—bare-looking, steep-sided, and sharply crested—drops precipitously away from the peak.

East of the ridge the vista is almost all new. From left to right you'll see Mt. Angeles, Klahhane Ridge, and, at the end of the ridge, the great gray hulk of the well-named Rocky Peak. Directly below you the Hurricane Ridge Road curves across the meadow, and below the road the steep slopes of Cox Valley plunge down to Morse Creek. In the distance is the long crown of Blue Mountain (Walk No. 8 and 9). To the right of Blue Mountain are three summits on the eastern arm of Hurricane Ridge: Green and Elk mountains and Maiden Peak. Still farther to the right you may glimpse parts of the gravel road to Obstruction Point, as well as Steeple Rock and Eagle Point, on the northeast side of the road.

The spur trail to Sunrise Point is the most exciting part of the Walk. Meadows slope steeply away on both sides of the narrow path, and the views get better and better as you climb higher and higher. When you reach Sunrise Point, you'll be at the highest point of the Walk—almost 5,500 feet. The panorama includes a sweeping view of the Olympic Mountains to the south; Mt. Angeles is less than a mile away.

After you've absorbed the view, retrace your steps to the four-way junction and follow the trail straight ahead, which climbs up to Alpine Hill. (If you were taking Walk No. 5 [Klahhane Ridge] you'd take the trail to the left.)

Just a couple of hundred feet from the intersection you'll be on Alpine Hill's 5,471-foot summit. Climb up on the large rock to the left of the trail and

*Open subalpine meadows along the **Hurricane Ridge Nature Trails** (Walk No. 2) provide stunning views of the Lillian River Valley. The valley's steep slopes are intertwined like the interlocking fingers of two hands. Snow-flecked Olympic summits are on the horizon.* ▶

enjoy another panoramic view—especially the sweep of snowy Olympics to the south. And comfort yourself, if you like, with this fact: Your climbing is over; the rest of the Walk is either level or downhill.

You'll barely start descending Alpine Hill on the crest of a wide ridge when you'll suddenly come face to face with a stunning view of the Lillian River Valley and the steep, creased tree-covered ridges rising steeply on both sides of it.

Then the path switches back and forth and brings you to a point, furnished with a bench, from which you can enjoy another view of the Lillian Valley and two more steep valleys—those of the Elwha River (Walk No. 13) and Long Creek—to the west. You'll also have a wide view of Hurricane Ridge and other landmarks to the east. And on clear days you can even see the Cascade Range, more than 30 miles away.

About .1 miles from the top of Alpine Hill, the trail is paved again. About .2 miles from the summit you reach an intersection. Take a left and almost immediately you'll come to another intersection. Go right and, as you follow the Big Meadow Loop Trail to the west, you'll have continuous views of the Olympic peaks to the south.

In another .2 miles you'll come to another intersection. If you're in a hurry you can take a left and be back at the parking area in less than .1 miles (and the visitor center in about .2 miles). If you have time for another view from the edge of the cirque, take a right and you'll quickly come back to the Cirque Rim Trail. When you reach the trail, go left and enjoy the stunning vistas again as you retrace your steps to the parking lot.

3 Wolf Creek Trail

This easy .3-mile round trip follows the eastern end of the Wolf Creek Trail through a wildflower-filled meadow with uninterrupted views of the Elwha Valley and snow-dappled Olympic peaks.

The Walk begins on the Hurricane Ridge Road, about 18.9 miles beyond the park entrance and about .7 miles past the Hurricane Ridge Visitor Center. There are small parking turnouts on both sides of the road. From the right (north) side of the road you can see a half-dozen landmarks, including (from left to right) the green meadows on Hurricane Hill (Walk No. 4), which from here look as smooth as a golf course; Unicorn Peak and Griff Peak in the Elwha River Range; the deep valley of the South Branch of the Little River; the long, thin arm of Ediz Hook reaching from Port Angeles into the Strait of Juan de Fuca; and the craggy hulk of Mt. Angeles towering over the valley on the right. In the distance, across the strait, is Vancouver Island, in British Columbia. On a clear day you can see buildings in Victoria, the island's largest city.

The trail begins on the opposite side of the road. The path was once an unpaved road linking Hurricane Ridge to the Elwha Valley; in fact, before the present Hurricane Ridge Road was opened in

the late 1950s, it was the only way you could reach the ridge by car. Today the upper end of the trail is a wide, smooth track, perfect for strolling side by side. It traverses a meadow that plunges into a forest of subalpine firs. In summer, the path is bordered by large, exuberant sweeps of fragrant lavender lupine, plus more modest displays of scarlet Indian paint-brush, yarrow, pearly everlasting, and even a patch of wild strawberry near the beginning of the trail.

Across the meadows to the left you have continu-ous views of the Elwha River and Long Creek valleys, whose slopes drop more than 4,000 feet. On the horizon are Olympic summits topped with snow. To the right is the large glacier on 6,995-foot Mt. Carrie. This trail is the closest Great Walk to Mt. Carrie and has the clearest view of the peak.

Less than 700 feet from the trailhead, the path runs into the woods and the views disappear. At that point you can turn around and walk back to your car.

The Wolf Creek Trail, incidentally, is little used by day hikers, so on most days you're apt to have it all to yourself.

4 Hurricane Hill

This moderate 3.5-mile round trip takes you up 5,757 foot Hurricane Hill on a paved path that goes almost all the way to the summit.

◄   *The Wolf Creek Trail (Walk No. 3) provides continu-ous views of the glacier-covered 6,995-foot massif of Mt. Carrie.*

Because you'll be walking through open sub-alpine meadows, your views of major Olympic landmarks will be continuous, and they'll get wider and wider as you ascend. At the top of Hurricane Hill, the panorama includes Mt. Olympus and the Bailey Range to the south, Port Angeles and the Strait of Juan de Fuca to the north, Mount Angeles and Klahhane Ridge to the east, and the Elwha Valley to the west. Signs explain the fascinating character-istics of this rugged subalpine environment and point out the literally dozens of summits you see from the trail.

The Walk begins at the end of the Hurricane Ridge Road, about 1.4 miles beyond the Hurricane Ridge Visitor Center and about 19.6 miles from Port Angeles. (See pages 20-25 for a description of the road.) The trail starts at the western end of the park-ing area. The first half-mile is nearly level, so it's handicapped-accessible.

At first the trail runs dramatically along the nar-row crest of Hurricane Ridge. Wildflowers decorate both sides of the path, meadows dotted with sub-alpine firs plunge steeply on both sides of the trail, and you have views in almost every direction. Behind you and to your right are summits along the southern rim of the Little River Valley. The panora-ma, from left to right, includes the pointed hulk of 6,454-foot Mount Angeles, the flat-topped Klahhane Ridge, the bare Rocky Peak, Sunrise Point, Sunrise Ridge, Alpine Hill, and the Cirque Rim Trail (Walk

No. 2). On your left and almost perpendicular to the trail are the V-shaped valleys of (from left to right) the Lillian and Elwha rivers and Long Creek. Rising above the valleys are snow-covered mountains, including the glacier-covered slopes of Mt. Carrie and Mt. Fairchild and the summits of Mt. Ferry, Mt. Fitzhenry, Mt. Scott, and other peaks of the Bailey Range. Behind the Bailey Range are the glaciers of Mt. Olympus. Ahead of you, in the west, are Mt. Appleton and Boulder and Everett peaks.

Soon the trail leaves the crest of Hurricane Ridge and follows its southern slope. Here the path is a corniche, a long, level linear terrace carved out of the steep meadow. Now you have only occasional views to the north, but uninterrupted vistas of snow-flecked gray peaks to the south.

Then the trail starts climbing—steeply at first, then more gradually—as it passes patches of pearly everlasting and scrubby mountain ash with clusters of bright orange-red berries. To your left, the steep slopes of the meadow plunge down to river valleys hundreds of feet below. South of the valleys you can glimpse white-water streams tumbling down mountainsides. (Binoculars will give you a clearer picture.)

Now the trail curves to the right and passes through a shady stand of subalpine fir before emerging again onto an open meadow. The trail then climbs more steeply as it bends to the right again and approaches the west rim of the cirque at the head of the upper Little River Valley. The last time we were here—a bright early August day—an enormous 100-foot-long snow patch lingered to the right of the

trail. Farther down the valley a black bear ambled across the manicured-looking meadows.

From here to the summit, the trail climbs gently but continuously. To make the climb as easy and enjoyable as possible—and to best appreciate the views—go slowly and rest as often as you like.

As the trail switches back and forth, across and up the wide open meadow, your views become wider and wider and more and more summits come into view. In the west, you'll see the pointed Lizard Head Peak and Happy Lake Ridge, just south of it. The first time we were here—a warm day in September— a golden eagle flew off the top of a subalpine fir and soared toward the sun.

About .2 miles from the summit, the Elwha-Hurricane Hill Trail (which leads to the Elwha Valley [pages 82-95]) joins the path on the left.

A couple of hundred feet farther, a spur trail on the right takes you quickly to an overlook at the edge of the steep valley of the South Branch of the Little River. From here you can see both the Cirque Rim Trail (Walk No. 2), at the southern end of the valley, and the beginning of the Hurricane Hill Trail, now more than 600 feet below. East of the valley you can see Mt. Angeles, Sunrise Point, Sunrise Ridge, and Alpine Hill. A plaque here identifies 28 other landmarks that stretch from Blue Mountain (Walks No. 8 and 9) in the east to Happy Lake Ridge in the west.

◄ *The summits of Mt. Olympus, Mt. Ferry, Stephen Peak, and other snowy promontories rise from the Elwha River Valley, south of* **Hurricane Hill** *(Walk No. 4). Lavender lupine and other wildflowers bloom in mid-summer.*

Follow the spur trail back to the main trail and almost immediately you'll come to the edge of a steep slope that plunges precipitously northward. A plaque explains the vista, which ranges from Unicorn Peak, Unicorn Horn, and Griff Peak, all in the Elwha Range, on the left, to Port Angeles and the Strait of Juan de Fuca in the center, to Mt. Angeles and Klahhane Ridge on the right. On a clear day you can see British Columbia on the other side of the strait, the San Juan Islands to the northeast, and Mt. Baker and other Cascade peaks in northern Washington.

From here a short unpaved path leads to the top of Hurricane Hill, where the views are even better. From the rocky summit you can see Baldy Ridge and its highest summit, 4,680-foot Mt. Baldy, to the northwest, and you have a raven's-eye view of Port Angeles, including ships in Port Angeles Harbor and the skinny three-mile-long peninsula known as Ediz Hook. This is obviously a terrific spot for lunch.

When you're ready, follow the path back to your car.

If you want to extend your walk, you can follow the Elwha-Hurricane Hill Trail to the edge of the ridge about .2 miles from the main trail. You'll have continual views of Mt. Olympus and other peaks to the south, and you'll walk through a tranquil meadow, thick with lupine and other blooming wildflowers in the summer.

5 Klahhane Ridge

This moderately strenuous 9.2-mile round trip is a grand tour. As you walk on or near the crest of both Sunrise and Klahhane ridges you'll be more than a mile above sea level and you'll have continuous panoramic views of virtually every landmark in the area, from snow-covered Olympic summits to the Strait of Juan de Fuca. You'll traverse one of the lushest wildflower-filled meadows on the peninsula, and you'll enjoy close views of craggy Mt. Angeles and a bird's-eye vista of Lake Angeles.

Like Walk No. 2 (the Hurricane Ridge Nature Trails), this Walk begins on the north side of the parking area adjacent to Hurricane Ridge Visitor Center, about 18 miles from Port Angeles on the Hurricane Ridge Road. (See pages 20-25 for a description of the road.) The trail starts near the eastern end of the parking area, about .2 miles east of the visitor center (and on the opposite side of the road) and just a couple of hundred feet west of the junction of the Hurricane Ridge and Obstruction Point roads.

Since the first .4 miles of this Walk follow part of the route of Walk No. 2, you could easily combine both Walks by (1) following the route of Walk No. 2 as far as the Klahhane Ridge Trail junction, (2) taking the Klahhane Ridge Trail and the rest of the route of this Walk to its turnaround point on

Klahhane Ridge, (3) returning to the Klahhane Ridge Trail junction, and (4) following the remainder of the route of Walk No. 2 back to the parking area.

This Walk first follows a paved path through an open meadow, past profuse clusters of lupine, bistort, and other wildflowers. Within just the first .1 miles you'll come to three trail junctions. For the quickest and easiest route to the Klahhane Ridge Trail, go straight ahead at the first intersection, left at the second, and right at the third. From the third intersection to the four-way junction on top of Sunrise Ridge you'll follow the route of Walk No. 2; see pages 34-36 for a description.

When you reach the four-way junction, take the trail on the far (east) side of the ridge. (The path to the left follows a spur ridge north to Sunrise Point, just .1 miles away. The trail to the right climbs up Alpine Hill and then gradually descends to the trailhead; for variety you can take it on your way back to your car if you like.)

The trail to Klahhane Ridge is a smooth but narrow corniche carved into the steep slope of Sunrise Ridge. Its views to the north, east, and south (described on Walk No. 2 [pages 35-36]) are uninterrupted. In the open wildflower-dotted meadows you can see the path stretch far ahead of you. Bare of trees, the land hides nothing.

The path very gradually descends and, after passing through a cluster of subalpine firs, reaches a saddle on top of the ridge. Now you can see to the west again and the view, from left to right, includes Hurricane Hill, Unicorn and Griff peaks—all on the west side of the Little River Valley—and the Strait of Juan de Fuca and Vancouver Island to the north.

Then the trail climbs gently, either on or just to the right of the crest of the ridge. As the path goes farther to the east, more and more of the Olympics will come into view, and you'll see both Alpine Hill and Sunrise Point near the southern end of the ridge. You'll also have dramatic views into Cox Valley.

The trail then climbs steeply to a high point on the ridge. From here you'll see *over* the crest of the ridge to the south, so your view of snowy Olympic summits will be unbroken.

About 1.3 miles from the trailhead, you'll see a short side path on the left that takes you up quickly to the top of the highest point on the ridge. The views here are panoramic; you'll see everything you've seen on the Walk so far, but since your vantage point is higher, the vista will be even fuller. If you didn't have time to take the entire Walk, this would be a superb destination all by itself.

After you've enjoyed the view, retrace your steps back to the main trail. (Avoid the other trails on the knob; they're misleading and rough.)

Now the trail curves to the left, around the north side of the knob. The side path on the right goes to a viewpoint, about 100 feet from the main trail, from which you have a bird's-eye view of Cox Valley.

The main trail begins to descend between patches of heather and scarlet paintbrush and switches back and forth through subalpine firs. Then it levels off in an open meadow. You're now on the north side of Cox Valley and you'll see Steeple Rock on

the south side. North of the ridge you'll spot cliffs on the lower slope of Mt. Angeles. Farther ahead the Klahhane Ridge Trail zigzags up the slope of the meadow on the right. Below, on the right, is the parking area for the Switchback Trail (described below).

Next the trail follows the crest of the ridge, heading straight for the steep slope of Mt. Angeles. At the end of the ridge the path splits. The left-hand fork is the rough, steep trail up the precipitous slope of the mountain. The Klahhane Ridge Trail goes to the right, traversing a lush, steep meadow where white bistort and orange Columbia lilies bloom in July. You'll see more purplish-brown crags on Mt. Angeles on your left, Cox Valley on your right.

After passing in and out of groves of evergreens, the trail crosses a rocky, usually dry stream bed, where patches of snow linger as late as early August. Then you'll see the Switchback Trail parking area again, more than 700 feet below. Immediately after that—about 2.7 miles from the trailhead—the Switchback Trail leaves the Klahhane Ridge Trail on the right.

Follow the Klahhane Ridge Trail straight ahead through the lushest meadow on the Walk and one of the most extensive displays of wildflowers in the Olympics—vigorous clusters of bistort, Columbia lilies, cow parsnips, lupine, phlox, pink sweetpeas, paintbrush, and many others. Occasionally the path

◄ *The **Klahhane Ridge Trail** (Walk No. 5) is etched into Sunrise Ridge, whose smooth subalpine meadows are decorated with ragged drifts of subalpine firs. The rough hulk of the well-named Rocky Peak looms on the left.*

runs through clusters of subalpine firs—welcome shade on a warm day.

The path switches back and forth 12 times as it makes an arduous climb up Klahhane Ridge. Whenever it switches back to the left you have continuous views of crags on Mt. Angeles, rising to the west of the ridge.

About halfway to the crest of the ridge, you'll begin to see over Sunrise Ridge to the glaciers on Mt. Olympus and Mt. Carrie. As you climb even higher you'll see over Hurricane Ridge to the Needles and other glacier-capped peaks in the eastern edge of the park. You'll also have closer and closer views of the jagged, pointed crags on Mt. Angeles, which look almost like the ruins of a castle. As you approach the top of the ridge, the soil gets thinner and rockier, the firs smaller, and the wildflowers sparse.

Finally, 3.7 miles from the trailhead, you reach the 5,880-foot-high saddle on the rocky crest of the ridge. On the north side of the ridge, the almost vertical slopes of a vast, desolate shady bowl drop hundreds of feet. There are almost no plants there, and patches of snow linger until August. To the left are the ramparts of Mt. Angeles; look for the trail etched into the steep slope. Straight ahead is the Strait of Juan de Fuca and the Dungeness Spit. On the far side of the strait you can see Victoria on Vancouver Island. To the right of the island are the San Juan Islands, Mt. Baker, and other Cascade peaks. To your right you can see the Klahhane Ridge Trail running along the eastern arm of the ridge; beyond the ridge is the even steeper face of the well-named

Rocky Peak.

After you've enjoyed the view, start following the Klahhane Ridge Trail across the steep southern slope of the ridge. Turn around occasionally and, as you climb higher up the ridge, you'll see past Mt. Angeles to Hurricane Ridge, sweeping from Hurricane Hill to Obstruction Point.

Soon you'll come to a lovely grassy saddle with lots of pink-flowering pussytoes. From here you'll see the Port Angeles coastal plain, including the three-mile-long Ediz Hook stretching into the strait. You'll also see tiny Lake Dawn in the forest near the Heart O' the Hills Ranger Station. Farther along the trail you'll see the town of Sequim. The last time we were here, an early August afternoon, the path went across patches of snow. Even more snow was piled up near the top of the shady slope just north of the trail.

The path follows the crest of the ridge for about .2 miles, then runs through subalpine firs and junipers on the north slope. Now you'll see the plunging snow-flecked bowl below Mt. Angeles and the mountain's prickly northern spine.

Then the path descends slightly and you'll see the Dungeness Spit and Sequim to the left of the sprawling hulk of Rocky Peak. To your right you can discern the road on Blue Mountain (Walks No. 8 and 9) and the peaks on the eastern arm of Hurricane Ridge (Walk No. 6).

The trail returns to the ridge crest, where you'll have views to both the north and south. Then it climbs steeply up a rocky knob that's the highest point on the ridge. The path is narrower and rockier here and the footing sometimes loose, so watch your step. The view from the top, however, is panoramic.

From the knob the path descends past large clumps of lavender lupine, then through broad meadows of pink and white heather. Now you'll see not only Port Angeles and Sequim, but Mt. Douglas and Victoria on Vancouver Island and Mt. Baker and other Cascade peaks. Rocky Peak is on your right.

Keep following the path down through the meadow until, about 4.6 miles from the trailhead, you see Lake Angeles tucked into the base of the steep cliffs in front of you.

You've now seen the best views on the Walk, which is why this is a good place to turn around and follow the trail back to your car.

If you don't want to walk all the way back to the trailhead, here's an alternative: Take two cars and leave one of them at the base of the Switchback Trail on your way to Hurricane Ridge; on your return trip, keep following the Switchback Trail all the way down to the Hurricane Ridge Road. Below its junction with the Klahhane Ridge Trail, most of the Switchback Trail is in evergreen woods, so it has almost no views. But the lower part of the trail is only about .6 miles long, it's a quick and easy downhill jaunt, and it can cut 2.1 miles and a good chunk of time off your return route. The last time we took it,

*Yellow fan-leaf cinquefoil, scarlet paintbrush, and other colorful wildflowers bloom beside the **Obstruction Point-Deer Park Trail** (Walk No. 6) in mid-summer. The steep walls of Badger Valley, snow-dappled even in August, sweep up to 6,000-foot **Lillian Ridge** (Walk No. 7), on the left, and 6,450-foot Obstruction Peak, on the right.* ▶

we didn't have a spare car to leave at the base, so we asked someone to give us a ride back to the Hurricane Ridge Visitor Center parking area.

6 Obstruction Point-Deer Park Trail

This undemanding 5.4-mile round trip follows the highest trail in the Olympics over the highest part of Hurricane Ridge. As you walk more than 6,000 feet above sea level you'll have uninterrupted above-timberline views in every direction. The panorama encompasses snowy Olympic peaks, the beautiful Grand Creek Valley, the Strait of Juan de Fuca, and steep subalpine meadows flecked with snow even in summer.

Like Walk No. 7, this one begins at the end of the Obstruction Point Road, about eight miles from the Hurricane Ridge Visitor Center. See pages 25-28 for a description of the road.

Follow the left-hand path at the very end of the road, the one marked with the sign saying, among other things, "Badger Valley .3."

The trail curves to the left, traversing the east slope of Obstruction Peak; the often narrow path is scratched into the steep, almost bare wall of the promontory. On your right, the tiny headwaters of Badger Creek cascade down the headwalls of Badger

Valley. Farther to the right, Lillian Ridge (Walk No. 7) sweeps up the southwest side of the ravine. Straight ahead, the arid, tan bulk of 6,764-foot Elk Mountain, the highest peak on Hurricane Ridge, rises on the north side of the valley. You'll easily see the trail (which you'll be following in a very few minutes); it's a diagonal line amid tufts of grasses and wildflowers on the smooth, treeless mountainside. Because subalpine vegetation is fragile, the Park Service asks you to walk only on the trail and avoid trampling the plants.

Snow lingers as late as August on these shady eastern and northern slopes. The last time we were here large snowfields lay just below the crest of Lillian Ridge and along the upper slopes of the valley. The path itself crossed several deep snow masses; the Park Service had installed a rope across the largest one to help hikers get across without falling down the steep, slippery slope.

About .3 miles from the trailhead, the Badger Valley Trail goes off to the right and switches back and forth down the deep V-shaped ravine. Stay on the Obstruction Point-Deer Park Trail. On your left, the rough, steep cliffs of Obstruction Peak loom above the trail.

Now the trail begins to climb gradually. Just past

---

*The **Obstruction Point-Deer Park Trail** (Walk No. 6) provides continuous views of (from rear to front) Mt. Olympus, the highest mountain on the horizon, and other snow-covered summits of the Bailey Range; the snow-splotched **Lillian Ridge** (Walk No. 7); Badger Valley; and subalpine meadows decorated with lavender lupine in mid-summer.* ▶

the Badger Trail intersection, follow the 80-foot path on the left of the trail up to the top of a saddle between Obstruction Peak and Elk Mountain. There you'll have a sweeping view to the north, west, and south. From left to right the panorama includes Mt. Olympus, Mt. Carrie, and other peaks of the Bailey Range; Eagle Point, on Hurricane Ridge; Mt. Angeles, at the western end of Klahhane Ridge (Walk No. 5), and Rocky Peak. Directly below is the deep valley between Eagle Point and Obstruction Peak. Turn around here and you'll see more peaks to the southeast: Baldy, Gray Wolf Ridge, the well-named Needles, Mt. Deception, and other summits to the right.

You'll keep seeing the view to the east after you return to the main trail and gradually climb Elk Mountain. You may also see deer snoozing in the lusher lower meadows of Badger Valley. You'll also pass junipers and an amazing profusion of wildflowers of almost every color, including fragrant lavender lupine, scarlet paintbrush, Indian thistle, and silky phacelia. Many of them grow in long, narrow rows roughly perpendicular to the trail. The rows of flowers are separated from each other by parallel rows of bare, stony soil known as frost-patterned ground or rock streams. The rock streams, which look like erosion, are caused by frost or ice, which lifts the stones out of the ground. When the frost or

◄ *Clouds cover the west slope of Obstruction Peak and the tops of snow-covered Olympic summits, seen from the* **Obstruction Point-Deer Park Trail** *(Walk No. 6). The pink flowers of the sweet vetch bloom in the subalpine meadows along the path.*

ice melts, gravity pulls the stones downhill. This disturbance prevents wildflowers from taking hold.

As you get higher and higher up the mountain, you'll see more and more Olympic peaks to the south and east. Look behind you and you'll see large snowfields on the north side of Obstruction Peak.

About a mile from the trailhead, the trail becomes almost level as it continues along the south side of Elk Mountain. On your right, meadows seem to roll over the edge of the mountain before plummeting down the precipitous slope of Badger Valley. On both sides of the trail, perpendicular rows of wildflowers contrast dramatically with alternating rows of rocks covered with black lichen.

Soon you'll come to a saddle, from which you'll have your first views of the Olympic coast: the Sequim Prairie and the long, thin Dungeness Spit curving out into the Strait of Juan de Fuca, Vancouver Island and the San Juan Islands across the strait, and Mt. Baker and other Cascade summits to the northeast.

As you continue along the gentle trail, you'll see tiny cascades—wispy threads of white water—falling from melting snowfields on the north wall of Lillian Ridge.

A bit farther ahead you'll begin to see past the western end of Lillian Ridge and up Grand Valley. The valley is a lovely natural composition. Pale-green meadows surrounded by drifts of dark-green evergreen trees cover the relatively moist and gentle lower slopes. The meadows taper up to steep, brown, snow-dappled hills that resemble the coat of a piebald horse; the summits are crowned with

rough outcrops of brown-black rock. The crest of
the ridge to the left of the valley looks as thin and
delicate as a knife edge.

Like many great landscapes, Grand Valley also has
water. Grand Lake and the smaller Moose Lake, farther up the ravine, are emerald-green focal points.
Cascading Grand Creek is a slender white accent,
beautifully offset by the greens of the meadows and
the trees. In the distance are Baldy, Gray Wolf Ridge,
the Needles, and other peaks.

About 2.2 miles from the trailhead you come to
the Elk Mountain Way Trail, which goes down to
Badger Valley. Keep following the main trail straight
ahead. As you gradually descend to a broad saddle,
note the jagged, buttresslike cliffs on the right side
of the ridge.

The saddle soon narrows dramatically, and you'll
have views on both sides of the ridge. From left to
right the vista includes the Hurricane Ridge Visitor
Center; Hurricane Hill (Walk No. 4); Alpine Hill
and Sunrise Ridge (Walk No. 2); Unicorn Peak
(south of Hurricane Hill); Mt. Angeles, Klahhane
Ridge, Rocky Peak, and Burnt Mountain, all rising
above the Hurricane Ridge Road; Ediz Hook
enveloping Port Angeles Harbor; Vancouver Island
and the San Juan Islands; the Cascade Mountains;
the three pointed summits of Maiden Peak, the next
summit ahead of you on the ridge; and the lower,
tree-covered Green Mountain, to the right of
Maiden Peak. On the right side of the ridge you can
see (from left to right) Blue Mountain, Baldy, Gray
Wolf Ridge, the Needles, and other snow-flecked
peaks to the southeast.

About 2.7 miles from the trailhead, the path climbs up to a picturesque viewpoint on the crest of the ridge where low subalpine firs and cedars form a neat ground cover and snowfields on the shady north side of the crest linger until August.

Beyond this point, the trail drops into a low col before climbing back up to the flank of Maiden Peak. Beyond Maiden Peak, the trail begins its long, gradual descent to Deer Park (Walks No. 8 and 9). The path is often shrouded by trees, which hide the views, and the views are lower, less-impressive versions of those you've already seen. That's why this is a good place to turn around and enjoy the scenery from another perspective as you follow the trail back to your car.

One day we walked this trail when Badger Valley was filled with fog, and the treeless, moorlike meadows reminded us of Scotland.

7 Lillian Ridge

On this moderate three-mile round trip—the second-highest Great Walk in the Olympics—you'll walk on or near the crest of a 6,000-foot-high ridge where you'll have continual views of snow-flecked Olympic summits, plunging subalpine meadows, and a host of other landmarks, including Hurricane Ridge, Grand Valley, and Lillian Creek Valley.

Like Walk No. 6 (the Obstruction Point-Deer Park

Trail, which is the highest Great Walk in the Olympics), this Walk begins at the end of the Obstruction Point Road, about eight miles from the Hurricane Ridge Visitor Center. See pages 25-28 for a description of the road.

Take the right-hand trail at the very end of the road; you'll see it curving up the steep treeless slope of the ridge. Because plants at this elevation are very fragile, be sure to stay on the trail to avoid stepping on them. The last time we were here—a sunny early August day—there was still a large snowfield to the left of the path.

As you climb up the stony slope of the ridge, you'll see the Obstruction Point-Deer Park Trail etched into the seemingly bare wall of Elk Mountain, on your left. On your right are the snow-covered summits of the inner Olympics, dominated by the massif of Olympus itself. Pink heather, lavender asters, and low, skirted subalpine firs grow along the path, but on this part of the Walk there are more rocks than plants.

The path then traverses a scree slope near the crest of the ridge. On one of our visits there was a big snowfield here, about 60 feet wide and more than 200 feet long.

Then the trail crosses an unusually level flat, sev-

---

*The **Lillian Ridge Trail** (Walk No. 7) provides continuous views of: the summits of Mt. Olympus (left) and other Olympic peaks; subalpine meadows where pink mountain heather and other wildflowers bloom beside snow in midsummer; and (from rear to front) the valleys of Long Creek, the Elwha River, and two forks of the Lillian River, separated by long, sharp-crested ridges.* ▶

eral hundred feet wide, at the very top of the ridge. The plateau, thick with rosy pussytoes and other tiny wildflowers, has panoramic views — Mt. Olympus and its neighbors in the south; Obstruction Peak and Hurricane Ridge to the west; Hurricane Ridge and the Strait of Juan de Fuca to the north; the Cascades to the northeast; Baldy, Gray Wolf Ridge, the Needles, and Mt. Deception to the east. The plain is so high and so wide, and its views are so extensive, that it gives you a wonderful "top-of-the-world" sensation. It could be a terrific destination all by itself.

After crossing the flat, the path descends the steep south side of the ridge, switching back and forth amid a jumble of rocks on sturdy, sometimes elegant, steps made of large flat rocks. Now you have a sweeping view to the south and west, including the Lillian River Valley, dozens of Olympic summits, and a tiny lake, or tarn, to the right, below the trail. On your far right you can see the Obstruction Point Road, Hurricane Hill (Walk No. 4), and the green meadows around the Hurricane Ridge Visitor Center (Walk No. 2).

Then the trail traverses patches of pink-flowering heather in a rocky meadow on the south side of the ridge. Here you're apt to see and hear marmots and blue grouse. The last time we were here we were fascinated by three marmots wrestling with each other; like furry little sumo wrestlers, they kept trying to push each other over.

Next the path gently climbs up to the narrow crest of the ridge, where you'll have expansive views both north and south. Directly ahead of you, the steep east slope of the ridge plunges down to Badger Valley. The bluff is dotted with snowfields and tiny lakes; the long snowfield on the relatively shady upper slope, just below the crest, lingers til late summer. On the far side of the valley is the bare silhouette of Elk Mountain. To the right of Elk Mountain are the other summits on the eastern arm of Hurricane Ridge—treeless Maiden Peak and the lower, forested Green Mountain—on the north side of Grand Creek Valley. Look carefully and you may see people on the Obstruction Point-Deer Park Trail. To the right of Hurricane Ridge is Blue Mountain (Walks No. 8 and 9)—you can see the Deer Park Road ascending the mountain and the trees burned by the forest fire of 1988. You're now almost 6,400-feet high—high enough to see the Strait of Juan de Fuca and the San Juan Islands, and past Hurricane Ridge to Mt. Angeles and Klahhane Ridge (Walk No. 5). To the south you'll have continuous views of the brown, snow-dappled ridge on the south side of the Lillian River Valley.

The views continue as you make a dramatic but easy climb up the narrow spine of the ridge. As you walk you'll hear (but not see) tiny creeks cascading down the walls of Badger Valley. Soon you'll see a little emerald-green lake in the light-green meadow near the bottom of the ravine.

The trail leaves the steepening crest of the ridge and traverses its precipitous southern flank. Now you'll pass wildflowers—lupine, pussytoes, red heather, yarrow, bistort, lavender asters—growing in steep, narrow rows roughly perpendicular to the path and separated by rock streams (explained on pages 60-61).

About 1.4 miles from the trailhead, the trail curves to the left, around the knob on the crest of the ridge, and reaches a trail junction at the edge of a wide, deep saddle.

If you keep following the main trail for 100 feet or so you'll see two tiny lakes in the bottom of Grand Valley. On the east side of the valley, steep, smooth but creased walls sweep up to rocky caps. Farther to the east, gray snow-flecked peaks jut up to the sky; the most dramatic of all are the Needles, whose snowy peaks are like parapets above nearly vertical fortresslike walls.

Beyond this point, the trail descends into Grand Valley, which is why this a good place to turn around and follow the trail back to your car.

Deer Park

Walks No. 8 and 9, which offer uninterrupted vistas of Olympic summits, begin in the mile-high subalpine meadows near the end of the Deer Park Road in the northeastern corner of Olympic National Park.

The closest accommodation to the trailhead is Deer Park Campground. The nearest motels and restaurants are in Port Angeles, about 18 miles away

*The **Lillian Ridge Trail** (Walk No. 7) is etched into mile-high subalpine meadows bedecked with pink mountain heather and other wildflowers, and flecked with snow even in August. The view includes (from left to right) Mt. Cameron, Mt. Claywood, and McCartney Peak.* ▶

(see page 20 for information on accommodations).

Climbing almost to the top of 6,007-foot Blue Mountain, the **Deer Park Road** is the second-highest road on the Olympic Peninsula. Its sweeping views rival those from the Obstruction Point and Hurricane Ridge roads, the highest and third highest, respectively, on the peninsula.

The road begins on the south side of Route 101 by the Deer Park Cinema, about five miles east of downtown Port Angeles. It climbs gently past country houses and, about 7.4 miles from Route 101, becomes gravel. Here you'll see the treeless, grassy slope of Blue Mountain ahead and the snow-flecked summits of Hurricane Ridge off to the right.

At about 8.4 miles the road enters the national park and curves through sweeps of tall salal as it climbs the evergreen forest on the northwest slope of Blue Mountain. It soon becomes a smooth but narrow shelf, twisting in and out of creases on the precipitous slope. Through the trees on the right you'll have better and better views of the snowy crest of Hurricane Ridge, rising 4,500 feet above the bottom of the valleys of Maiden and Morse creeks.

About five miles beyond the park boundary the road is almost a mile high, the trees begin to disappear, and wildflower-filled subalpine meadows take their place. Now you'll have a dramatic 180-degree view to your right. Straight ahead, less than ten miles away, are major Olympic summits: from left to right, Grey Wolf Ridge, the Needles, 7,788-foot Mt. Deception, and Mt. Cameron. Just to the right are the peaks of the eastern arm of Hurricane Ridge

(Walk No. 6). Closest to the road is Green Mountain, whose tree-covered slopes are dotted with tiny meadows. Beyond Green Mountain is ledgy 6,434-foot Maiden Peak, its gently sloping light-green meadows so smooth that they look like immense lawns. Farther to the right is the Hurricane Ridge Road, cut into the slopes of (from left to right) Mt. Angeles, Klahhane Ridge (Walk No. 5), Rocky Peak, and Burnt Mountain. To the south, beyond Round Mountain, are Port Angeles, the Strait of Juan de Fuca, and Vancouver Island on the horizon. This view is especially dramatic because the mountains and ridges soar thousands of feet above the valley of Maiden Creek, which plunges down the steep meadow to the right of the road. In summer the meadows are speckled with bursts of fragrant lupine, creamy cow parsnips, scarlet paintbrush, and other flowers. From here til the end of the road, your view will be an ever higher, ever wider version of this one.

About 16.4 miles from Route 101, and again at 16.7 miles, the road forks. Go left at each junction. (The right-hand roads both go to the Deer Park Ranger Station.)

In about 16.8 miles you'll come to the entrance to the **Deer Park Campground** on the right. The road to the right of the signboard goes to the **Deer Ridge Trail** *(Walk No. 9)*.

The Deer Park Road now curves to the left, away from the campground, and climbs up the treeless western slope of Blue Mountain.

In another .9 miles the road ends at a parking area on the north side of the mountain. From here you can see ships in Port Angeles Harbor and, farther

east, the lighthouse near the end of Dungeness Spit. On a clear day you can see the San Juan Islands and the Cascades. Steep meadows dotted with clusters of sharp-pointed subalpine firs fall off to the north and east. On this dry, sunny summit, the grass is as thin and short as a sheep pasture's.

The Deer Park Road used to go to the top of Blue Mountain, but in the 1970s the Park Service wisely decided to end it here and turn the last couple of hundred feet into the first half of the **Rainshadow Nature Trail** *(Walk No. 8).*

8 Rainshadow Nature Trail

This undemanding .5-mile loop takes you gently to the summit of 6,007-foot Blue Mountain. No other Great Walk takes you so quickly and easily to an Olympic mountaintop or provides such sweeping summit vistas for so little effort. You'll enjoy awesome views of snow-flecked mountains and deep-plunging valleys along the entire length of the Walk. A well-

◀ *Steep subalpine meadows along the **Deer Park Road**, on the upper slopes of **Blue Mountain** (Walks No. 8 and 9), are spotted with the blooms of scarlet paintbrush, white cow parsnips, and other wildflowers in mid-summer. The Needles and other snow-draped Olympic summits sweep thousands of feet up from the valley floors.*

written six-page trail guide describes both the vistas and the fascinating characteristics of this "dry island above a sea of green."

The trail begins at the parking area at the end of the Deer Park Road, just below the summit of Blue Mountain. See pages 70-73 for a description of the road.

Pick up a trail guide in the box at the trailhead and follow the wide path (once part of the Deer Park Road) up the west side of the mountain. Your view to the right will be a higher and wider version of the vista you first saw from the Deer Park Road (described on pages 70-71).

The pamphlet explains that Blue Mountain is a "dry island" in a "sea of green" because Mt. Olympus, to the southwest, is a rain-and-snow filter; it takes more than 240 inches of precipitation from clouds moving across the mountains from the Pacific, thereby depriving the region to the north-east of moisture. As a result, Blue Mountain, in the "rainshadow" of Mt. Olympus, gets only 50 inches of precipitation per year, little more than one-fifth of what Mt. Olympus gets.

The pamphlet also explains how wildflowers have adapted to survive this fierce environment; why Olympic marmots, Olympic chipmunks, and a few other species are found here and nowhere else in the world; and how fires affect the color of the forests to your right (they burn off old dark-green Douglas fir stands, allowing new light-green trees to replace them).

The path makes a wide, counterclockwise sweep

around the summit of the mountain, where you can see even farther to the east. Left of the Gray Wolf Ridge is 6,797-foot Baldy; left of Baldy, in the Olympic National Forest, is 6,364-foot Tyler Peak. The last time we were here—a bright, windy midsummer afternoon—a soft fog drifted toward the summit, completely filling the valleys to the east. When the fog lifted, we could see steep meadows falling hundreds of feet toward Canyon Creek. These half-bare steppes look every bit as fragile as they are—as if they had been overgrazed by sheep.

As you head back toward the parking area, you see what the trail guide calls the "dinosaur-like ridge" on the north slope of the mountain. The rocky ridge crest is actually an outcrop of basalt that was uplifted millions of years ago.

As you walk down the mountain, the path winds neatly past handsome gardenlike sweeps of subalpine firs. The firs survive here because the north side of the mountain is shadier and less windy than the other slopes. With less wind and sun, the soil retains moisture, so plants get more water. Notice that the grass here is longer, thicker, and lusher than elsewhere on the mountain and that even corn lilies, which like wet meadows, grow in a few moist spots.

9 Deer Ridge Trail

This undemanding 1.5-mile round trip curves through open meadows on the south slope of Blue Mountain, providing nearly continuous views of the Gray Wolf Valley and Olympic summits to the south.

The Walk begins in the Deer Park Campground, near the end of the Deer Park Road (described on pages 70-73). To reach the trailhead, follow the road to the right of the signboard at the entrance to the campground, then take your second right, then your first left. The trailhead is about .1 mile from the signboard.

The smooth, nearly level trail starts crossing a lush, lupine-filled meadow and immediately forks. The right path goes into the campground. Take the trail to the left, which continues across the meadow. On your left is the south summit of Blue Mountain (Walk No. 8). On your right is the Gray Wolf River Valley and, rising up from the south slope of the valley, a long ridge of peaks, snow flecked even in summer. From right to left, the view includes Gray Wolf Ridge, the Needles, Mt. Deception, and Mt. Cameron.

After curving through a ravine, the trail briefly enters a grove of firs and comes to another fork. The right-hand path goes to Three Forks Campground, at the confluence of Grand Creek, Cameron Creek, and the Gray Wolf River. Follow the trail to the left, out of the firs and across the south slope of Blue Mountain.

The smooth, nearly level path is now a narrow track etched into the mountainside. The soil here is much thinner, rockier, and drier than that in the meadow; instead of lush grasses and lupines there are clumps of delicate wildflowers. The treeless slopes allow continuous views into the Gray Wolf Valley and the summits rising beyond it.

The trail crosses another ravine—a barren, rocky waste—passes occasionally through small clusters of subalpine firs and lodgepole pines, and curves to the left, along the south slope of Blue Mountain. Now you can see peaks to the south and even the snowy summits of the Cascades, 30 miles to the east.

After twisting through a third ravine, the trail starts to descend, and the view is blocked by more and more trees. This is a good place to turn around, walk back to the trailhead, and enjoy the vistas again from another direction.

Dungeness Valley

Walk No. 10, the **Upper Dungeness Trail,** is in the Dungeness River Valley, which is in the Olympic National Forest, south of the town of Sequim (pronounced *Skwim*) and just east of the northeast corner of Olympic National Park.

Accommodations in the area include more than a dozen motels and B&Bs in Sequim; campsites at the Dungeness Recreation Area, north of Sequim; and two national forest campgrounds (see below) not far from the trailhead. The Sequim Dungeness Chamber of Commerce (PO Box 907, Sequim, WA 98382; 800-737-8462, 360-683-6197) can give you more information. Sequim is just 17 miles east of Port Angeles, which has even more accommodations (see page 20).

10 Upper Dungeness Trail

This very moderate four-mile round trip is a treat. It's one of only two Great Walks in the Olympics that are close enough to a stream to provide continuous views of exciting rapids, cascades, and other white water. (The other is the Staircase Rapids Trail [No. 60], in the Hood Canal region.)

To reach the trailhead, take Route 101 to the Palo Alto Road, which is on the south side of the highway, about three miles east of downtown Sequim, .2 miles east of the road to the John Wayne Marina, and 1.5 miles west of Sequim Bay State Park.

The Palo Alto Road heads south, past woodlands, pastures, and private homes. About a mile from Route 101 you'll have views behind you of Sequim Bay and the Strait of Juan de Fuca. About seven miles from Route 101 the Palo Alto Road enters the national forest and becomes gravel.

At about 7.9 miles the road forks. Forest Service Road 2880 goes to the right, Forest Service Road 28 to the left. The **Dungeness Forks Campground** is a mile down Road 2880, at the confluence of the Dungeness and Gray Wolf rivers. To reach the trailhead, take a left onto Road 28.

In another mile the road forks again. Road 28 goes to the left, Road 2860 to the right. Take a right and follow the narrow road down into the

Dungeness River Valley. About 11 miles from Route 101 you'll pass the **East Crossing Campground** and see the Dungeness on your right. In another .9 miles the road crosses the river. As it climbs away from it, you'll have views of the Dungeness Valley to your right.

At about 13.8 miles the road forks again. Road 2870 goes to the right, Road 2860 continues on the left. Stay on 2860. Now the road climbs Maynard Peak, becoming a narrow, winding corniche cut into the mountain as it traverses the steep slope high above the Dungeness. The views of the deep valley over the precipitous slope to your left are continuous. The last time we were here—an unusual overcast July day—the road was clear, but thick white fog filled the valley.

About 18.7 miles from Route 101, the road forks again. Road 2860-120 goes to the right, Road 2860 to the left. Go left and follow 2860 down to the bottom of the valley. At about 20.2 miles you'll cross a bridge over Mueller Creek and in another .1 miles come to the trailhead parking area on the left. The trail begins at a signboard on the right side of the road, just before a bridge over the Dungeness.

The trail climbs briefly up the bank to the right, away from the river, then switches back to the left and follows the Dungeness upstream. At first the trail is high above the river as it goes through a second-growth forest, past large clusters of Oregon grape, salal, huckleberry, vanilla leaf, bunchberry, and twinflower. Gradually, however, the trail drops close to the river and enters a darker, more open woods of large Douglas firs three to five feet thick at

the base. The spacious forest makes it easy to see the Dungeness, which sometimes is just 10 to 15 feet from the trail. The aqua river often bristles with white water as it rushes noisily by. Numerous side paths take you to streamside views.

About .9 miles from the trailhead you'll pass through an impressive stand of trees: an unusually thick grove of large Douglas firs. Immediately after it you'll come to a lovely, gardenlike woods where Royal Creek enters the Dungeness. Follow the short path on the left to a campsite beside the river and you'll walk through a woodland so clean and open that only needles and moss cover the ground between the trees.

Go back to the main trail and just a couple of hundred feet farther you'll be at a trail junction just before the long log bridge over the wide, cascading Royal Creek. The Dungeness Trail goes straight ahead; you'll follow it later. Right now go right and follow the Royal Creek Trail upstream past a huge, mossy, cabin-size boulder on the left. The trail switches back to the right, then back to the left, as it gently climbs the steep bank above the creek. You'll pass the Lower Maynard Burn Trail, on the right (the path is named after a forest fire that destroyed virgin forest on Maynard Peak and other summits in the early 1930s); then you'll cross several small creeks tumbling down the steep slope toward Royal Creek. As you traverse the open forest, you'll have continual bird's-eye views of the wildly cascading creek to your left.

◄   *The **Upper Dungeness Trail** (Walk No. 10) crosses the wildly cascading Royal Creek.*

The trail gradually bends closer to the creek, and your views will be even clearer. The creek is smaller than the Dungeness, but its bed is steeper, so it has many more cascades.

About .5 miles from the trail junction, the trail enters the national park and starts curving away from the creek, so your views of white water start to disappear. This is a good place to turn around, follow the path back to the trail junction, and enjoy the views of Royal Creek from another direction.

After you return to the Dungeness Trail, cross the bridge over Royal Creek and savor its long upstream view of cascades and rushing water.

On the other side of the creek the trail passes a level, elegantly open campsite on the left and immediately curves close to the river. Again you'll have all-but-continuous views of the river through the dark, open evergreen forest.

About .5 miles from Royal Creek, the woods start becoming less open and the trail starts moving away from the river, so the water views slowly disappear. When that happens, turn around and, as you follow the trail back to your car, appreciate the lively river from another perspective.

Elwha Valley

Walks No. 11-13 and **Honorable Mention No. 1** all begin in the lower Elwha River Valley, in the north-

*The glacier-covered peaks of Mt. Carrie and Mt. Fitzhenry tower over the Elwha River, which crackles over its rocky bed along the **Olympic Hot Springs Road**.* ▶

central part of Olympic National Park.

The closest accommodations to the trailheads are Elwha Campground (see below) and Altaire Campground (see page 315). The nearest motels and restaurants are in Port Angeles, about ten miles northeast of the Elwha entrance to the park (see page 20).

* * *

To reach the trailheads, take Route 101 to the **Olympic Hot Springs Road,** which is about eight miles southwest of downtown Port Angeles, three miles west of the intersection of routes 101 and 112, and eight miles east of the junction of 101 and the East Beach Road, at the eastern end of Lake Crescent (see page 96). As you approach the Olympic Hot Springs Road you'll have good views of the craggy western wall of the Elwha Valley.

About a mile up the Hot Springs Road you'll have your first views of the Elwha River, on your right, and the crags above the opposite bank.

The park entrance station is about two miles up the road, and the trail to **Madison Falls** *(Walk No. 11)* begins at a parking area just to the left of the station.

Just after the entrance station you'll have more views of the Elwha. Here the aqua river spreads 150 feet wide and splits around a long island in the middle of the current as it crackles over its rocky bed. Here, too, you have your first views, up the valley, of summits in the northern Bailey Range: 5,948-foot Mt. Fitzhenry and 6,995-foot Mt. Carrie, snow covered year round.

About a mile beyond the entrance station you'll pass **Elwha Campground,** on the left. About .8 miles after the campground you'll reach the **Elwha Ranger Station,** a charming collection of gray cedar-shingled buildings, built in the 1930s, on both sides of the road.

About .1 miles after the ranger station, on the left, is the **Whiskey Bend Road** (see below), which takes you to the **Upper Lake Mills** and **Elwha River trails** *(Walks No. 12 and 13)*.

The Olympic Hot Springs Road ends at the trail to the **Olympic Hot Springs** *(Honorable Mention No. 1)*, about 6.3 miles from the ranger station. The road (described on pages 315-316) is worth taking for its own sake because it passes several dramatic views of the Elwha and Lake Mills.

* * *

After leaving the Hot Springs Road, the unpaved, twisting **Whiskey Bend Road** immediately passes stables, on the left, and climbs sharply up the east wall of the Elwha Valley. The road is a narrow shelf carved into the steep, tree-covered slope, and the grade drops precipitously on the right. Drive carefully.

After about half a mile the road becomes less steep; at about .6 and .9 miles you pass waterfalls cascading down the bank on your left.

At about 1.4 miles you'll start seeing Lake Mills through the trees on the right.

At about 3.7 miles you'll pass another waterfall, on the left, and .4 miles later you'll reach the trailhead for the **Upper Lake Mills Trail** *(Walk No. 12)*, on the right; it's marked by a sign saying "Lake Mills."

In another .3 miles the road ends at a parking area at the beginning of the **Elwha River Trail** *(Walk No. 13)*.

11 Madison Falls

This very easy .2-mile round trip is a delightful stroll through a meadow, past giant bigleaf
maple trees, and along a pretty stream to a
woodland niche where a soothing falls trickles
and splatters down basalt cliffs.

The Walk begins at a paved parking area on the
left (east) side of the Olympic Hot Springs Road, just
past the park entrance station and about two miles
from Route 101.

The wide, paved, wheelchair-accessible path begins in the northern end of the parking area (the
end nearest the entrance station) and curves
through a meadow dotted with bigleaf maple trees.
Because the maples are in full sun, with no competi-
tion from any other trees, they've grown into beautiful giants with 50-foot-wide crowns and two- and
three-foot-thick moss-covered trunks; the largest
specimen, to the right of the trail, is six feet thick at
ground level. To the left of the walkway is a huge hollow trunk, almost three feet high and nine feet wide,
which looks like a large wooden tub.

Then the trail enters an evergreen forest, almost
immediately comes to Madison Creek, on the left,
and follows the creek upstream. The path curves to
the right and quickly ends at a long terrace at the
bottom of a steep slope that plunges down the right

◀ *Madison Falls (Walk No. 11) trickles and splatters*
down a mossy basalt cliff in the Elwha River Valley.

side of the trail. Madison Falls is straight ahead, trickling and splattering 30 feet down a basalt cliff decorated with moss and maidenhair ferns.

The terrace is a comforting place, nicely enclosed by the steep slope on the right and, on the stream side, by a handsome stout fence made out of four-by-six-inch rails. It's a fine spot for a long, lingering look at the falling water.

When you're ready, follow the path back to your car.

12 Upper Lake Mills Trail

If Lake Mills is low enough, this moderate one-mile round trip will take you down to the banks of the Elwha River, where you'll see one of the most exciting cascades in the Olympics.

The falls are on Wolf Creek near the point where the Elwha River flows into Lake Mills. Their accessibility depends on the height of the lake. If the lake is low enough you can walk along the banks of the Elwha to Wolf Creek and the base of the falls. If the lake is too high, it inundates the river banks, and the path to the falls ends not at the banks of the river but at the edge of the lake, and your route to the falls is blocked by the water. Inquire about the height of the lake before you take this Walk.

Lake Mills is created by the Glines Canyon Dam

(see page 315) across the Elwha River. Federal agencies are considering removing the dam to allow salmon once again to swim up the Elwha. If and when the dam is destroyed, Lake Mills will disappear too and the falls will *always* be accessible.

The Walk begins on the Whiskey Bend Road (described on page 85), about 4.1 miles south of its junction with the Olympic Hot Springs Road. Both the trail and the small trailhead parking area, marked by a sign saying "Lake Mills," are on the right (west) side of the road.

The trail enters an open second-growth woodland, immediately passes through a tall patch of salal, then switches back to the right and begins a long traverse of the steep slope above the Elwha. The trail passes more salal as well as drifts of ferns and mahonia as it makes several long switchbacks on its way down to the river.

Soon you'll hear Wolf Creek cascading down the slope to the north of the trail. You won't see the creek yet, but its sound will get louder as you walk closer to it, and it'll be loudest where the trail makes its first switchback to the left.

As you approach the last switchback, you'll hear the dull roar of the Elwha. When Lake Mills is low enough, the path ends at campsites on the flat, damp, sandy banks of the river, which are often dotted with deer tracks. The wide, shallow aqua river makes little bits of white water as it rushes by. Dead trees and logs, washed downstream, pile up against gray gravel bars and islands thick with willows. Across the river, splotches of the steep forested walls of the valley have been stripped bare by landslides.

Follow the Elwha downstream. In about 100 feet you'll come to Wolf Creek, which has carved out a two-foot-deep channel in the gravel beside the Elwha. Follow the creek upstream into a 50-foot-long gorge with 30-foot walls festooned with moss, ferns, salal, and bigleaf maples. The canyon ends at a mossy, moist, shady grotto, about 40 feet wide and nearly as high, almost totally encircled by near-vertical walls covered with ferns and young cedar trees.

In the center of the grotto, Wolf Creek shoots 25 feet down a ledge in a thick, powerful horsetail of white water that crashes onto the ledge near the bottom of the fall and splashes into a stony pool below. The cascade is one of the most exciting in the Olympics, falling with such speed and force that it resembles a giant faucet turned on full blast. Look carefully at the cascade and you'll see another, smaller falls behind it that begins about two-thirds of the way up the ledge. Set in the grotto like a diamond in a ring, the whole cascade is a splendid natural fountain. Unfortunately, the last time we were there logs leaning against the walls of the grotto marred the beauty of the spot. If they were washed farther downstream, the setting would be perfect.

The grotto is a fine spot for a picnic, or at least a long pause, before following the trail back to your car.

13 Elwha River Trails

This moderate 5.8-mile excursion offers an

assortment of treats: the dramatic Elk Overlook above the Elwha Valley; a bird's-eye view
of the Elwha surging through the rocky gorge
known as the Goblin Gates, plus several other
close views of the river; two interesting old cabins; and trails edged with handsome solid, gardenlike carpets of evergreen salal, mahonia,
and ferns.

The Walk begins at the parking area at the end
of the Whiskey Bend Road (see page 85), about 4.4
miles from the Elwha Ranger Station and 6.3 miles
from the park entrance station. Look for the sign for
the Elwha River trails at the southern end of the
parking lot.

At first you follow the Elwha River Trail, a wide,
often level path cut into the east wall of the steep-
sided Elwha Valley. A former roadbed, the trail is
one of the smoothest tracks in the park.

The route goes through a pleasant, open evergreen forest, past three- and four-foot-thick Douglas
firs and through beautiful solid evergreen carpets of
salal, mahonia, and ferns. Through the trees on
your right you'll have occasional glimpses of the dramatic steep west slope of the valley. Sometimes you'll
hear the rocky river below.

After about .9 miles you'll come to the short path,
on the right, to Elk Overlook. (It's marked by a sign
saying simply "Overlook.") The path switches back
and forth down the steep bank and, about 700 feet
from the main trail, comes to a pleasant, sunny aerie
with the Walk's first glimpse of the Elwha. The river,

here flowing bright white, is more than 400 feet below. On the west bank is a broad meadow that was the site of the Anderson Ranch; Roosevelt elk often graze here. Beyond the meadow is the steep, tree-covered west slope of the valley.

After you've enjoyed the view, walk back to the main trail.

About one mile from the trailhead you'll come to the northern edge of an area burned by a forest fire in 1977. The point is marked by a giant boulder resting precariously on the right side of the path. Notice the broken trunks of burned conifers and the shiny green leaves of young madrona trees, which thrive in the sunny clearings made by the fire. With no large trees blocking the way, you now have more views of the river and the western slope of the valley off to the right.

In another .1 miles you come to the Rica Canyon Trail, on the right, which takes you down to the river bottom. At first the trail runs directly down the steep slope of the bank (be glad you're going downhill) and leaves the burned area behind. Then it switches back to the right and enters one of the most soothing landscapes on the Walk: a cool, moist, mossy shelf, or bench, above the river. After strolling through a flat, shady woods, past green moss-covered logs and thickets of club moss, you'll gently descend to the river, whose roar gets louder as you get closer.

About .5 miles from the main trail you'll come to another intersection, just a few feet from the river. Take the delightful trail to the right, which hugs the river and provides continuous views of white water surging over its gravelly bed and the open meadow on the opposite bank.

In barely .1 miles the trail ends on a massive sandstone outcrop about 20 feet above the river. (There's no fence here. Be careful and hold children's hands.) You're now on top of one of the Goblin Gates. The "gates," one on each side of the river, are so close together—barely 15 feet apart at one point—that they abruptly force the Elwha into a deep, narrow, turbulent channel. From here you can see the Elwha flow up to the gates, swirl around the jutting rocks and—in an instant—change from a wide, shallow, frothing white river into aqua pools that are almost as deep as they are wide. This is the most exciting spot on the Walk and a superb place for lunch or a very long linger.

When you're ready, retrace your steps to the last intersection, go straight ahead, and follow the Geyser Valley Trail through a thick, wet forest of Douglas firs, vine maples, and bigleaf maples. The path follows the Elwha at first, then bends away from it. (To stay on the main trail, go left at any intersection; right-hand paths take you to campsites along the river.)

About .5 miles from the Goblin Gates the trail again runs close to the Elwha and traverses a steep bank above it. Here you'll have aerial views of the river and a long, low island covered with a grove of white-colored alders.

Then the trail climbs through evergreens, crosses a level woods carpeted with light-green club mosses, and, about .9 miles from the Goblin Gates, reaches another intersection. The left path (the Krause

Bottom Trail) goes back to the Elwha River Trail; the right path goes to the Humes Ranch.

Take the right trail, which switches back and forth down to a moist, flat, evergreen grove whose floor is covered with mosses. About .2 miles from the last intersection you'll come to several pleasant campsites beside the river.

Then the trail climbs back up into evergreen woods, where you'll have more bird's-eye views of the river through the trees on your right.

The path soon emerges onto a small meadow above the river. After crossing a tiny creek you'll come to another intersection. Straight ahead, at the far end of the meadow, and about .7 miles from the last trail junction, is a primitive two-room log cabin built in 1900 by two homesteaders, Will and Grant Humes. The Humes brothers also built a barn, planted an orchard, raised crops, hunted cougars, and guided hunters, climbers, and other early travelers through the region. Grant Humes went back East in 1914, but Will lived here until he died in 1934. The Park Service preserves the Humes Ranch as an example of a pioneer homestead.

After you've explored the cabin, follow the trail that climbs up into the forest on the east side of the meadow. (As you face the meadow from the front porch of the cabin, the path will be on your right.) You'll soon pass, on your left, the trail that runs directly up from the meadow (you passed it earlier). Then you'll recross the tiny stream you crossed at the edge of the meadow. The creek tumbles down the steep ledge on the left side of the trail in a long series of tiny cascades.

After passing large Douglas firs and thickets of mahonia, you'll come to another trail junction about .3 miles from the Humes Ranch. Go left (actually straight ahead).

The trail immediately levels off and, about .5 miles from the Humes Ranch, brings you to the Michaels Cabin, on the left. This one-room structure is a tad more elaborate than the Humes cabin. There's a dry sink and a loft inside, a shed on the back side, a long porch in front, and all the floors are wood. The cabin is named after E. O. Michaels, who lived near here at the turn of the century and was known as "Cougar Mike" because he hunted wildcats. The cabin, however, was actually built by two other men, Jay Gormley and Gus Peterson, in 1937. It was restored by the Park Service in 1980. Note the scenic alder meadow beside it.

Now follow the wide, smooth Elwha River Trail all the way back to the trailhead, which is about 1.8 miles from the Michaels Cabin. En route, you'll pass four other paths joining the trail on the left—the Krause Bottom Trail, the Rica Canyon Trail, and the two side trails to Elk Overlook. Go straight ahead at every intersection.

Lake Crescent

Walks No. 14-16 and **Honorable Mention No. 2** all begin at Lake Crescent, on the northern edge of Olympic National Park and about 18 miles west of Port Angeles.

Accommodations near the trailheads include two resorts and a campground (all described below) on the shores of the nine-mile-long lake.

To reach the trails, take Route 101 to Lake Crescent. The highway follows the southern shore of the lake for its entire length except for Barnes Point (see below). The road is seldom more than two or three yards from the water, so it provides continuing views of the lake and the mountains that rise dramatically all around it. Several parking turnouts, some with interpretive signs, make terrific lakeside picnic sites. Small waterfalls, some of them ephemeral, splash down the steep slope on the south side of the road.

* * *

If you drive to Lake Crescent from the east, you'll come to the junction of Route 101 and the **East Beach Road** about 18 miles from Port Angeles and eight miles west of the Olympic Hot Springs Road into the Elwha Valley (pages 82-95).

About .8 miles up the East Beach Road is the sandy **East Beach,** which also has a picnic area.

About 3.3 miles from Route 101 is the **Log Cabin Resort,** a park concession on the north shore with a splendid view of 4,500-foot Mt. Storm King (Walk No. 16), on the opposite side of the lake. Open April through October, the resort (360-928-3325) rents motel rooms, A-frame chalets, housekeeping cabins, rustic cabins, and RV trailer sites. There's also a restaurant, a small store, a sandy beach, and boats for rent.

If you drive west on Route 101 from its junction with the East Beach Road, you'll quickly come to the south shore of Lake Crescent. Barnes Point (see below) is about four miles from the junction.

* * *

If you drive to Lake Crescent from the west, you'll come to the junction of Route 101 and the **Camp David Jr. Road,** on the left, about .2 miles from the western end of the lake, 17 miles east of the junction of Routes 101 and 113, in Sappho, and 28 miles from the town of Forks.

Just about .2 miles up the Camp David Jr. Road is **Fairholm Campground,** which has RV sites (but no hookups) and a beach on Lake Crescent.

At the end of the road is the western end of the **Spruce Railroad Trail** *(Honorable Mention No. 2).*

Just .2 miles east of the junction of Route 101 and the Camp David Jr. Road is the **Fairholm Store,** a park concession at the western tip of the lake open from April to October. The store snack bar serves light meals, including breakfast. You can eat inside or at outdoor tables with excellent views down the lake to Mt. Storm King.

About 2.5 miles east of the store is **La Poel,** a lovely large, evergreen-shaded picnic area on the lakeshore.

About 4.2 miles past LaPoel is the road to **Barnes Point** (see below).

* * *

Walks No. 14-16 all begin at **Barnes Point,** which juts into the southern edge of Lake Crescent. The Barnes Point Road begins on Route 101, about 22 miles west of Port Angeles, 11.7 miles west of the Hot Springs Road into the Elwha Valley (pages 82-95), and 6.7 miles east of the Fairholm Store, at the western end of the lake. The junction is marked by signs for Lake Crescent Lodge, Olympic Park Institute, Marymere Falls, etc.

Turn onto the road and almost immediately you'll come to a four-way intersection. The road to the left goes to **Lake Crescent Lodge** and the **Moments in Time Trail** *(Walk No. 14)*. The road to the right goes to a large parking area at the beginning of the trail to both **Marymere Falls** *(No. 15)* and **Mt. Storm King** *(No. 16)*; both Walks start at a signboard to the right of attractive, well-scrubbed rest rooms with flush toilets. The **Storm King Ranger Station** is just a few yards down the trail.

Built in 1914-15, **Lake Crescent Lodge** rivals Lake Quinault Lodge (see page 230) as the most beautiful accommodation on the Olympic Peninsula. Its immense lobby—36 feet wide, 14 feet high, and almost 60 feet long—is one of the largest rooms in the park. Finished with dark wood and furnished with handsome mission furniture, the grand rustic hall also has a huge, 12-foot-wide fieldstone fireplace.

The lodge's pièce de résistance, however, is its sun porch. The room is 12 feet wide and 60 feet long, and almost its entire north and east walls are windows—a stunning tapestry of more than 1,000 panes of glass set in a delicate-looking membrane composed of yards and yards of white wooden mullions. The glass wall alone makes the porch the most impressive bit of architecture in the park. At a time when windows are made of vinyl mullions and other synthetic materials, this fenestration is a magnificent, precious monument to quality, taste, and architectural integrity.

The windows provide a sweeping view of Lake Crescent and allow the white walls of the porch to be bathed in light, even though the room is on the northwest side of the lodge. The porch is furnished with white wicker furniture, whose delicacy complements that of the windows, and decorated with large pots of geraniums and other light-loving plants.

The lodge's most attractive acommodations—*mirabile dictu!*—are also its cheapest. They're the five guest rooms on the second floor. They're finished with wooden floors and (real) wooden paneling and furnished with upholstered wooden furniture. Most important, the north wall of each room is dominated by a large, beautiful 24-pane casement window that provides both a splendid architectural focal point and a wonderful water- and mountain-filled view of the lake and Pyramid Mountain on the opposite shore. The rooms are inexpensive mainly because they have no baths (just a sink); they share two showers, two sinks, and two toilets in four different rooms across the hall.

Also attractive are the Roosevelt Cottages, built in the 1920s and named for President Franklin Roosevelt after he visited the park in 1937. At the very edge of Lake Crescent, the spacious cabins have fieldstone fireplaces, warm wooden floors, paneled walls and ceilings, and wide views across the lake.

The lodge also offers more modest cabins as well as motel-type units in three different "motor lodges" on the grounds; many of these have lake views too.

The lodge dining room isn't as handsome as the

rest of the lodge (it was added much later), but the tables near the large windows in the northwest wall have great views of the lake. Tasty, moderately priced meals are served three times daily.

A national park concession, the lodge (416 Lake Crescent Rd., Port Angeles, WA 98363-8672; 360-928-3211) is open from late April to late October. The Roosevelt Cabins, however, are also rented, on weekends only, from early November to late April at a discounted rate.

14 Moments In Time Trail

This easy .8-mile Walk is one of the best interpretive trails on the peninsula. It offers long shore-side views of Lake Crescent, and its interesting signs, illustrated with full-color paintings, describe both the human and natural history of the area.

You can reach the Moments in Time Trail—a wide, smooth .7-mile loop—on five different paths, but the approach with the best views begins at Lake Crescent Lodge. (See pages 97-98 for directions to the trailhead.)

Park in the lot just east of the lodge, walk across the grass to the edge of the lake, and savor the vista. Barnes Point is at the narrowest part of Lake Crescent—the lake is just half a mile wide here—and you can see the crags above the Spruce Railroad Trail (Honorable Mention No. 2) on the opposite shore. (Binoculars will bring the view even closer.) Rising above the crags is the well-named 3,000-foot Pyramid Mountain. Off to your left, more than five miles away, is the western end of the lake, which rests at the bottom of a V-shaped valley formed by forest-clad ridges rising steeply from both the south and north shores. The ridge on the north side of the lake drops gracefully, rhythmically to the valley at the western end in a series of five summits, each one lower than the one to the east of it. The slopes of each summit are almost parallel, and the hills on both sides of the water appear to be braided together like the interlocking fingers of two hands.

After you've enjoyed the view, follow the meadow along the lakeshore, away from the lodge, and look for a sign saying "Storm King Ranger Station." About 100 feet beyond the sign you'll see a smooth, gravelly path that curves between large evergreen trees and past thick sweeps of St. Johnswort, whose bright yellow flowers bloom in early summer.

You'll barely start following the path before you come to three rows of half-log benches arranged in a rough semicircle around a fire ring at the edge of the lake; rangers give evening talks here around a blazing fire.

At this point the trail splits. Take the path to the left, which immediately enters a shady evergreen forest; ferns and Oregon grape grow along the trail.

The path quickly reaches the Moments in Time Trail. To follow the loop clockwise, take the path to the left, which runs close enough to the lake so you can see it through the trees. Signs along the way describe bald eagles, black-tailed deer, river otters, and other indigenous animals. They also note that Lake Crescent has two varieties of trout, Beardslee rainbows and Crescenti cutthroats (named, of course, for the lake), that are found nowhere else in the world.

Less than .1 miles from the start of the loop, the trail comes out of the woods at a beach at the tip of Barnes Point. From here you can see the whole length of the lake. Signs explain how the Spruce Railroad was built on the far side of the lake to haul spruce lumber to build airplanes during World War I. Although the railroad was built in "record time"—five months—the war ended before it was finished. (For more on the railroad, see page 132.)

Next to the beach is a pleasant grassy meadow dappled with clusters of cedars and Douglas firs. As the trees get bigger and more numerous, they're gradually turning the meadow back into an ever-green forest. Signs here point out that the valley of Lake Crescent was carved by a glacier, that the lake was created when landslides formed a natural dam at its eastern end (about 15,000 years ago), and that Barnes Point is actually a delta of Barnes Creek, which carried rocks, sand, and silt from the mountains south of the lake and deposited them on the shore.

Now the trail runs briefly along the lake before coming to another junction. The left path goes to the nonprofit Olympic Park Institute, which sponsors environmental-education programs. A trail sign here explains that the institute was once the site of

Rosemary, "a rustic inn bordered by several hand-crafted cabins." Opened in 1914, Rosemary was named for its founder and owner, Rose Littleton, and her lifelong assistant, Mary Daum. Rosemary's early guests took a ferry to Port Angeles and then rode a touring car to East Beach on Lake Crescent; from there they would sail to Rosemary on either the *Marjory* or the *Storm King*, two paddlewheel ferries that plied the lake. President Franklin Roosevelt ate breakfast at Rosemary in the fall of 1937. During the Great Depression, however, tourism declined, and Rosemary hosted its last guests in 1942. The inn was sold to the park the following year and placed on the National Register of Historic Places in 1979. You can glimpse some of the old resort buildings through the trees on the left of the trail.

Take the path to the right at this and the next three intersections.

The trail now curves through a lush evergreen forest and past six-foot-thick stumps, evidence of early 20th-century logging. A sign in front of one unusually large stump—ten feet wide and six feet high—explains how lumberjacks used springboards to lift themselves above the "buttressed bases" of large trees (see page 132 for an explanation of "high stumping"). Notice the holes, cut into the tree, into which the ends of the springboards were inserted.

Another sign, in front of a fallen Douglas fir, notes that the dead tree is a "nurse log for a new generation of trees." The cedar and hemlock trees growing on the mossy log may one day become a row, or colonnade, of trees, with their "roots encircling the shape of the vanished nurse log." (Nurse logs, which are a medium for young trees to grow in, are also discussed on pages 216-217.)

After passing more giant moss-covered logs and large drifts of sword ferns, you'll reach a huge moss-covered Douglas fir snag, or standing dead tree, to the right of the path. The fir grew to an incredible 15 feet wide at its base before its top broke off. Another Douglas fir across the trail is ten feet thick at its base. A sign here says both trees are between 300 and 700 years old.

The trail then enters a grove of red alders. A sign explains that they're "pioneer species" that grow in "disturbed soils" (such as flood plains) but are eventually shaded out by hemlocks and cedars, which grow much taller than alders and, as a result, absorb most of the sunlight in the forest.

Another sign, farther along the trail, identifies a cedar, a hemlock, and a ten-foot-thick Douglas fir and explains that the "multi-layered canopy" provided by these evergreens "shelters wildlife from rain, wind and sun."

Next you'll come to a large cedar almost completely burned out on the inside. The charred hole is 5 feet wide and 20 feet tall, as big as a small teepee. A sign explains that the tree is still alive because its live tissues survived the fire. Ironically, the inside of trees is often more susceptible to fire than the outside, because the inner wood is dead. The living cells are all close to the bark.

The trail enters another alder meadow dotted with a few bigleaf maples. A sign in front of one bigleaf maple blanketed with mosses announces that the mosses are epiphytes—plants that get their food and water from fog and rain—and that they're not parasites, as you might think; on the contrary, the trees send their roots directly into decomposed layers of moss to get food and water from *them*.

Now the trail curves along the edge of the meadow you passed earlier on the Walk. According to a sign here, it was the site of a homestead in the early 1900s. Painted on the sign is a fetching picture of a white dormered farmhouse with yellow-green trim, an unpainted barn and other outbuildings, and what looks like a Model T Ford parked in front of the house. Although, according to the sign, the meadow is being "kept open by grazing Columbia black-tailed deer," young Douglas firs are already starting to turn it back into a forest. As recently as the late 1990s the meadow was still open enough to show the lake in the distance.

Finally, the trail passes a red cedar snag to the left of the path. The dead tree is still standing, according to a sign here, because of its "long-enduring buttressed base." The holes in the trunk were "carved by fire" and provide nesting sites for such creatures as Naux's swifts, owls, bats, flying squirrels, martens, and even wood ducks.

Now you'll quickly come to the junction where you began the loop trail. Take a left here, retrace your steps to the parking lot near the lodge, and enjoy the views across the lake from another perspective.

15 Marymere Falls

This very moderate two-mile round trip takes you to one of the two most intriguing cascades in the park. En route you'll have views of Lake Crescent and Barnes Creek and you'll walk through a mature forest with lots of giant evergreens.

The Walk begins at Barnes Point on Lake Crescent. See pages 97-98 for directions to the trailhead.

The trail begins as a paved walkway that runs along the edge of a daisy-filled meadow with a view of the lake to the left. Almost immediately you come to the Storm King Ranger Station, a handsome log cabin with a fieldstone fireplace and warm woodwork inside. The building may look old, but it's actually a re-creation of the original station built by a ranger in the early 1900s. The first building stood beside Route 101 and was destroyed in 1979 when a bulldozer fell off a tractor trailer and crushed it.

From the ranger station, a wide, smooth gravel path curves into the woods and immediately splits. The left fork goes down wooden steps to the lapping waters of the lake, where you'll have a wide view of its northeastern shore. The right fork, which is wheelchair accessible, follows a level route through the woods and rejoins the left fork in a couple of hundred feet.

Then the path goes through a tunnel under Route 101 and emerges at a meadow on the other side of the road. To the right of the trail is an enormous double-trunked bigleaf maple with a broad crown spreading luxuriously over the grass.

The trail, now as wide as a road, runs through a mossy evergreen forest; you'll pass many large Douglas firs, some of them six feet thick at the base. The steep slope of Mt. Storm King (Walk No. 16) rises on the left; Route 101 is on the other side of the trees to the right.

About .4 miles from the ranger station you'll pass a trail to Lake Crescent Lodge on the right. Then you'll come to a huge Douglas fir, on the left, that's an amazing 12 feet wide at its base. Very soon after that you'll pass the Mt. Storm King Trail, also on the left. Beside the intersection is an enormous boulder, about 40 feet across at its widest point and about 25 feet high at its tallest; moss, ferns, and even small trees grow on top of it.

Immediately after the trail junction the path runs close to Barnes Creek, on the right, and you'll have your first view of the 30- to 40-foot-wide stream flowing briskly over its rocky bed.

Shortly after that, the path forks again. The Barnes Creek Trail goes straight ahead; the falls trail goes to the right. Take a right. Almost immediately you'll pass a giant cedar whose impressive nine-foot-wide base reaches to the very edge of the trail.

Now the path approaches Barnes Creek and curves to the left. Before you follow the trail upstream, walk to the edge of the creek for another view of the rushing stream and the long, low gravel island in the middle. On the far side of the creek you'll see a log bridge over the mouth of Falls Creek,

which flows into Barnes Creek. You'll cross the bridge shortly.

First, however, you'll walk briefly upstream and cross another bridge—a large, picturesque 30-foot log—over Barnes Creek. The span provides long views, upstream and downstream, of the shallow creek churning over its stony bed.

On the other side of the bridge you'll pass an intriguing hollow log and immediately cross the bridge over Falls Creek. Look up the creek and you'll see some of the cascades below Marymere Falls.

After crossing the stream you'll climb its steep bank on wooden steps. Through the trees on your right you'll have an aerial view of Barnes Creek.

The trail switches back to the left, then back to the right by a wooden bench. Immediately after the bench the trail splits into a loop. The right path goes directly to the falls' upper viewpoint. The left trail goes to the lower viewpoint first.

Take the left path, which is cut into the precipitous wall of the gorge below the falls; a stout log fence prevents you from accidentally slipping over the edge. Here you have uninterrupted views of the creek cascading over ledges 50 feet below. Cedars, hemlocks, and ferns flourish on the moist, mossy walls of the ravine.

You'll walk along the shelf in the gorge for a couple of hundred feet before you'll see the falls

◀ *The moss-covered roots of a massive Douglas fir line the narrow path cut into the steep gorge below 75-foot* **Marymere Falls** *(Walk No. 15), near Lake Crescent.*

through the trees ahead. The images here are overwhelmingly vertical; the long, narrow stream of falling water echoes both the high, precipitous walls of the ravine and the tall, straight trees thrusting up from them. As you move along the narrow path in the long, narrow canyon, the sense of great height imposed on great depth makes you almost giddy.

Soon you'll come to a viewpoint about 60 feet away from the rocky base of the falls. So much water crashes with so much force that the air here is thick with mist. Photographing the falls is all but impossible here because you can't keep your lens dry.

For a drier view of the falls, climb the long flight of wooden steps behind you and you'll come to the upper viewpoint, opposite the midpoint of the 75-foot-high cataract.

The torrent leaps out of a notch in the steep, dam-like ledge at the head of the canyon. Some of the water shoots so far away from the ledge that it falls almost all the way to the bottom before crashing into the rock.

Unlike, say, the cataract on Wolf Creek (Walk No. 12), Marymere doesn't fall in a solid column of water. If you look at just one part of the fall as it starts its descent and keep watching it as it drops, you'll see that the top two-fifths or so of the cascade is really a cluster of large falling fragments of water. The bottom three-fifths are sheer gossamer layers of mist and minifalls.

Unlike other falls, Marymere doesn't make a constant dull roar. Instead its thick sheets of water go thwack, thwack, thwack as they crash, one after the other, on the ledge; then they make a shooshing sound as they splash into the 20-foot-wide gray-green pool at the base of the falls. Notice that moss grows only around the lower two-thirds of the cascade. That's because the upper part of the ledge is almost always dry; an overhang at the top of the ledge shields it from rain. Note also how the color of the moss depends on its proximity to the falls, and how maiden hair ferns grow on the outer edge of the moss.

Marymere rivals Rocky Brook (Walk No. 52) as the most intriguing cascade on the peninsula. Take time to enjoy it before following the path back to your car.

16 Mt. Storm King

This somewhat strenuous 4.2-mile round trip takes you up the steep slope of Mt. Storm King, the 4,500-foot peak that dominates the eastern end of Lake Crescent. You'll enjoy frequent and sometimes dramatic views of Lake Crescent and the mountain ridges rising sharply from its shores. You'll also pass giant evergreen trees and luxurious sweeps of salal.

Like the Walk to Marymere Falls (No. 15, above), this one begins at Barnes Point on Lake Crescent. See pages 97-98 for directions to the trailhead.

Begin the Walk by following the trail to Marymere Falls (page 106). About .4 miles from the Ranger Station you'll see the Mt. Storm King Trail beside a gigantic mossy boulder on the left.

The path immediately begins switching back and forth up the mountain. The smooth but narrow path, etched into the steep slope, is flanked by salal, Oregon grape, twinflower, and the long, thin moss-covered branches of vine maples. You'll hear (but not see) Barnes Creek in the valley below.

After the fifth switchback you'll catch a glimpse of the west end of Lake Crescent through the trees. Then the path goes between two giant Douglas firs, both five feet thick at the base; then it switches back to the left, then back again to the right. Now you'll have even better views of the lake and of 3,000-foot Pyramid Mountain rising above the north shore. You've also climbed high enough to see over the tops of trees and across Barnes Creek Valley.

The trail then switches back to the left and crosses a small flat where a luxurious unbroken sweep of three-foot-tall salal carpets the floor of a grove of Douglas firs four to five feet across at their bases.

Now the path climbs more gently, through a woods so dark that only needles carpet the floor, then through a grove of giant Douglas firs as much as six feet wide at their bases, and through more tall salal on both sides of the trail.

The path skirts the rim of the precipitous north slope of the mountain and switches back to the right. At the switchback you have a bird's-eye view of Barnes Point (including the parking area near the Storm King Ranger Station), the east end of the

Mt. Storm King (Walk No. 16) rises nearly 4,000 feet above Lake Crescent. Drifts of white daisies decorate the western shore. ▶

lake, and the low, craggy hills above the northeastern shore. Notice the different colors of the lake—aqua near the shore and in shallow bays, bluer in deeper or shaded water.

The path now climbs more steeply through a lovely, open woods, past more tall salal, four-to-six-foot-thick Douglas firs and young hemlocks whose green foliage contrasts beautifully with the brown furrowed bark of the firs. Here, through the trees, you'll have more glimpses of the western end of the lake.

After curving through more sweeps of salal the path emerges in a clearing at the edge of a sunny bluff where manzanitas and madronas grow. Now you have a wide-open view across Barnes Creek Valley to Aurora Ridge, the 10-mile-long spine that parallels the southern edge of the lake. The ridge is topped, like a dragon's back, with a long row of little pointed summits. You can also see a bit of the lake to the right, and you can still hear Barnes Creek, more than 2,000 feet below.

At the clearing the trail switches back to the left and climbs steeply up the crest of a spur that drops off on each side of the path. Look back for occasional views of Aurora Ridge.

The trail now makes a long traverse of the steep south slope of the mountain, passing solid sweeps of salal on both sides of the path. Ahead of you is a mossy crag you'll come to in a few minutes.

Then the trail switches back to the left, then to the right, then back to the left again. Before following the trail to the left at the last switchback, however, follow another path to the right of the trail. In about

50 feet you'll come to the crag you saw earlier. There you'll have a more easterly view of Barnes Creek Valley and Aurora Ridge. This part of the ridge is higher than the crest you saw before, and its peaks are flecked with snow even in midsummer.

Go back to the main trail, which climbs through open, sunny woods and soon comes to the crest of a dramatically narrow ridge on the north face of the mountain. One side of the ridge drops steeply to the south; the other plunges even more precipitously to the shore of Lake Crescent, more than 3,000 feet below. (Watch your step here because the north face of the mountain is a sheer drop.) From this skinny aerie you can now see beyond the eastern slope of Pyramid Mountain, on the far side of the lake, to the Strait of Juan de Fuca and Vancouver Island. You'll also have an eagle's-eye view of Route 101, almost directly below you, at the bottom of the mountain and parallel to the curve of the lake. Here too you can see the many hues—aquas, blues, and purples—of the eastern end of the lake. A few yards to your right you can see the basalt cliffs on the north face of the mountain, as rough as the ones you're standing on. Look behind you and, through the young trees, you'll have another view of Aurora Ridge.

The trail now bends sharply to the right and starts climbing the knife-edge spine of the sunny open ridge. The panorama expands with every step. Almost immediately you'll be able to see all of Pyramid Mountain, then (behind you) the western arm of the lake and most of the eastern end; then you'll be high enough to have an unobstructed view of Aurora Ridge. A few feet more and you'll see

almost the entire twisting shore of the lake, nearly surrounded by steep, tree-covered hills plunging straight down to the water.

After following the crest for about 100 yards, the trail runs through a beautiful mossy border and reenters the woods. At that point, a path on the left climbs quickly back up to the wooded crest of the ridge. (This trail is not maintained and there is no fence at the edge. so use extreme caution.) Here you'll have the best lake view on the Walk: a sweeping vista of virtually all of Lake Crescent, including Lake Crescent Lodge and the ranger station on Barnes Point, the shallow aqua water along the east side of the point, and the long row of peaks running west from Pyramid Mountain.

After you've enjoyed the vista, return to the main trail, which traverses the southern slope of the mountain until it switches back to the left at a small clearing. From there you'll have another sweeping view—to the western end of Lake Crescent and across Barnes Creek to Aurora Ridge. You'll keep seeing this view as you follow the trail to another sharp turn to the left.

After passing a lovely large moss-covered ledge on your right, the path switches back to the right to climb farther up the rock. You'll catch a glimpse of the lake through the trees before the trail switches quickly back to the left, then to the right again, and emerges on top of a rocky knoll fringed with

◀ *Mt. Storm King (Walk No. 16) provides dramatic aerial vistas of Lake Crescent and the mountains rising steeply from its shores.*

madrona, manzanita, salal, ocean spray, and uncommon patches of bearberry.

From this perch you have views of the lake through the trees, and you'll be able to see farther up the Barnes Creek Valley than you could anywhere else on the Walk. A sign here announces that this is the end of the "maintained trail" and that "steep cliffs and rough terrain beyond this point" make further "travel hazardous."

This is obviously an excellent spot to stretch out and enjoy a long, leisurely lunch before turning around and looking at the views again on your way down the mountain.

Sol Duc Valley

Walks No. 17-20 are in the Sol Duc River Valley, in the northwestern corner of the Olympic Peninsula.

Walks No. 17-19 are in Olympic National Park. To reach the trailheads, take Route 101 to the **Sol Duc Road**, which is 1.9 miles west of the Fairholm Store, on the western end of Lake Crescent (see page 97); about 15 miles east of the junction of Routes 101 and 113 in Sappho; and about 26 miles northeast of Forks. Accommodations along the road include a large campground and a resort (see below).

You'll follow the Sol Duc Road only .2 miles from Route 101 before reaching an interesting and attractive exhibit on the right; several large, elaborate illustrated signs describe the natural features of the region. About .2 miles farther you'll pass the entrance station, and about five miles from Route 101 you'll enter a lush, stately forest of large old evergreen trees.

About 6.8 miles from Route 101 you'll see your first view of the Sol Duc River, on the right; at about 7.3 miles you'll reach the **Salmon Cascades** *(Walk No. 17)*, also on the right; and at about nine miles you'll come to the **Ancient Groves Nature Trail** *(Walk No. 18)*.

About 12.2 miles from Route 101 you'll reach the **Eagle Ranger Station,** on the left. Built by the Civilian Conservation Corps in 1935 (see Walk No. 57), the rustic wooden building is one of the handsomest structures in the park. Its weathered gray-green cedar siding is nicely offset by mustard-colored wooden doors and windows. Its most impressive feature, however, is a pair of very large mullioned windows on the left front facade. Each window is divided into 15 panes of glass, three on the upper sash, 12 on the lower. Together they comprise a striking tapestry of mullions with an astonishing total of 30 panes of glass. The windows are flanked by wooden shutters that are not merely decorative but are large enough to cover the windows completely. The windows are perfectly centered in the left front facade, like a picture in a mat and frame; and, like a good frame, the facade offsets them well. With their large, mustard colored shutters, the windows have enough presence to offset the mustard-colored door on the right front facade; so even though the entire front facade is asymmetrical, it's nicely balanced.

Just past the ranger station, on the right, is **Sol Duc Hot Springs Resort,** a national park concession with three large outdoor pools fed by natural hot-mineral-water springs. The resort also has cabins, several with kitchenettes; a restaurant; a small grocery store; a gift shop; an outdoor swimming pool; and RV campsites. The resort (360-327-3583) is open from late May through late September.

Just past the resort is the **Sol Duc Campground,** which has several sites on the Sol Duc River.

Finally, about 1.3 miles beyond the campground and 14 miles from Route 101, the road ends at a vast parking area at the beginning of the trail to **Sol Duc Falls** *(Walk No. 19).*

* * *

Walk No. 20, the **Pioneer Path,** is in the Klahowya Campground, in the Olympic National Forest, about 9.6 miles west of Lake Crescent on Route 101.

17 Salmon Cascades

This very easy .1-mile round trip, through a deep, shady old-growth forest of huge mossy trees, brings you to exciting cascades on the Sol Duc River where countless salmon once leaped upstream.

The Walk begins in a parking turnout on the right side of the Sol Duc Road, about 7.3 miles from Route 101.

Follow the wide, level path between two giant Douglas firs, both six feet thick at ground level, then through a moist, shady evergreen woods where moss covers the ground and the trunks of the large evergreens and hangs like beards from the branches.

About 100 feet from the road you'll come to a wooden deck above the Sol Duc where you can watch the river surge down long chutes in a broad ledge that spans the stream. The largest cascade, more than 70 feet long, pours into a foaming 12-foot-wide channel and then into a 25-foot-wide aqua pool bounded by ledge walls on each side of the river.

A sign here explains that salmon once leaped over these cascades as they swam upstream in early autumn; now, thanks to over-fishing and habitat loss, they're seldom seen.

Take the path to the left of the overlook, follow it upstream for about 70 feet and you'll come to a ledge at the edge of the water where you'll be able to see about 200 feet up the cascading river.

After you've enjoyed the view, retrace your steps back to the parking area.

18 Ancient Groves Nature Trail

This easy .5-mile loop winds through a forest so old and dark that only moss and sword ferns grow on its floor. You'll see centuries-old Douglas firs, some as much as 11 feet wide at ground level. You'll have a bird's-eye view of the sparkling Sol Duc River, and you'll stroll around lovely woodland pools whose water-loving plants create beautiful green accents in the dark woods.

The Walk begins on a parking turnout on the right side of the Sol Duc Road, about nine miles from Route 101. A sign here explains why the endangered spotted owl needs old-growth forests to survive. The large trees "shield the spotted owl from predators such as the great horned owl"; branches shelter it from wind, rain, and snow; "broken tree tops and trunk hollows far above the forest floor" provide nests; and standing dead trees are home for flying squirrels, which the spotted owl eats.

A six-page trail guide, available in a steel box at the trailhead, eloquently describes much of what you'll see on the Walk. It notes that this lowland forest, like other Sol Duc Valley woodlands, shares many features of temperate rain forests nearer the Pacific coast, including a few Sitka spruces and bigleaf maples and rows, or colonnades, of evergreen trees growing out of large decaying fallen trees known as nurse logs. The trail enters the woods and almost immediately crosses a wet area on a bridge. Wetlands are one of the brighter parts of an old-growth forest because trees can't grow in them and consequently more sunlight reaches the forest floor. Because of the extra light, thick drifts of lady ferns and sword ferns thrive here.

After the bridge, however, the woods grow dark. As the trail guide explains, with some understatement, the tree canopy "filters sunlight, keeping undergrowth relatively sparse." Mosses and a few sword ferns are almost the only plants able to grow on the otherwise bare forest floor.

The smooth path winds past large western hemlocks and huge Douglas firs growing on little knolls; many of these hillocks may be the remains of nurse logs on which the trees first sprouted hundreds of years ago.

The trail quickly reaches the edge of a steep bank above the Sol Duc River. You can't see the river yet because red alders are in the way, but you can hear the low surging of the water more than 50 feet below.

The path bends along the edge of the bank, past large hemlocks and a big Douglas fir more than eight feet wide at ground level. Then you'll cross a bridge over a streamlet, and suddenly you'll have a bird's-eye view of the Sol Duc and the steep forested slopes on the opposite side of the valley. Here the river is flowing toward you, so you can see several hundred feet upstream. From this vantage point, the river is an intriguing, surrealistic sight. It shimmers and twinkles and emits a low whoosh as it churns over its rocky bed, but somehow it doesn't look as if it's flowing.

The trail then runs slightly below the rim of the bank, and you'll walk beside and almost under a boulder that seems to be resting precariously on the precipitous slope. How much longer, you wonder, before it obeys the law of gravity and rolls down the bank to the river?

The trail returns to the top of the bluff and comes alongside a crescent-shaped pool in a shallow depression in the forest floor. When we were here last—a late-July afternoon—the pool was about 25 feet wide and 100 feet long, but just a few inches deep. Growing along its edge were bleeding hearts and skunk cabbage, whose enormous, dark-green leaves make it look like very large hostas.

The path crosses the tiny outlet of the pond on a wooden bridge. Off to the right, the streamlet flows between soft beds of moss and over the edge of the bank toward the river.

Then the path runs along the edge of a much larger pool to the left and crosses its narrow end on another wooden bridge. From this vantage point above the water you can see that the pool is about a foot deep. Skunk cabbage and bleeding hearts grow in the shallow edges, and thick sweeps of fern flourish on the banks. The plants are a striking green accent in the middle of the somber brown woods.

On the other side of the bridge the trail forks. Take a left. (The right-hand path ends at the parking turnout a few yards beyond the trailhead.)

The loop trail runs briefly along the edge of the pool but then curves away from it and goes by one of the largest Douglas firs on the trail—11 feet wide at ground level.

Then you'll cross a tiny stream on a wooden bridge. Look downstream, to your left, and you'll see the bridge on which you crossed this tiny creek earlier on the Walk.

You'll pass more big Douglas firs, including a ten-foot-thick specimen on the left, before the path completes its counterclockwise loop by winding back into itself a couple of hundred feet from the trailhead. Go right at the junction and retrace your steps to your car.

19 Sol Duc Falls

This very moderate round trip, which can be as short as 2.2 miles or as long as 2.8, takes you through an attractive evergreen forest to one of the park's most exciting falls. En route you'll see a pretty cascading creek, a handsome rustic shelter built by the Civilian Conservation Corps, and a gardenlike section of woodland. After viewing Sol Duc Falls, you'll have bird's-eye views of the cascading Sol Duc River, and you'll see more falling water on Canyon Creek.

The Walk begins at the very end of the Sol Duc Road, 14 miles from Route 101. (See pages 118-120 for a description of what you see along the road.)

The trail begins by a signboard at the end of the vast, .1-mile-long parking area at the end of the road. You'll immediately pass giant evergreen trees and enter a spacious forest of big Douglas firs and young hemlocks. The well-groomed trail, one of the most popular in the Olympics, is wide, very smooth, and almost level.

Less than .1 miles from the parking lot the trail intersects the path, on the right, that leads to the Sol Duc Campground. If you have time, follow this trail as far as the Sol Duc River, only about .2 miles away. That part of the path is almost as smooth as paving, and the plants along the trail grow in clean, garden-like sweeps. The sides of the path are carpeted with moss, a swath of bunchberry grows behind the moss, huckleberry bushes rise beyond the bunchberry, and large old-growth trees loom in the distance. Unfortunately, the trail is much less interesting after it reaches the river, so turn around there and walk back to the main trail.

About .2 miles beyond the Sol Duc Campground Trail you'll cross a large wooden bridge over a pretty creek that tumbles over a bed of moss-covered rocks. The moss and the white water make a stunning contrast. You can watch the stream from a bench conveniently built into the middle of the bridge.

In another .4 miles you'll cross a small cascading creek and immediately come to a trail junction. Follow the trail to the right to Sol Duc Falls.

Just beyond the trail junction, on the left, is the Cabin Creek Shelter, built by the Civilian Conservation Corps (see Walk No. 57) in 1939. As a plaque outside the shelter notes, the structure is an "excellent example of Rustic Style architecture." Although technically just an open, one-room shelter, it's a delight to look at and, in fact, ranks with the Lake Crescent and Lake Quinault lodges as one of the handsomest buildings in the region. It's elegantly proportioned and generously framed with big logs; the stone-and-concrete fire ring in front is protected by a portico made of massive logs; and although it's a rustic structure "built of native materials, in scale with, and sensitive to, its immediate surroundings" (in the words of the plaque), it also has some stylish classical details: the portico is perfectly centered on the long side of the building, and, just like a Greek temple, the top, or gable end, of the portico and the gable ends of the main shelter are finished with (triangular) pediments. No doubt about it: the "CCC boys" had class.

The trail now follows a wooden railing down to the river. On your right you can see white water foaming between the mossy walls of the gorge below the falls.

You'll quickly reach a stout wooden bridge high above the river, where you'll have your first view of the falls and the long, deep, narrow gorge into which they flow. The crashing water makes so much mist that the bridge is soaking wet.

For the best view of the falls, cross the bridge and walk upstream, along the handsome log fence at the edge of the gorge, until you're opposite the cascades. Unlike most streams entering a gorge, the Sol Duc doesn't simply flow over the head of the ravine (the point farthest upstream). Instead, most of the river rushes past the head and, in a foaming, five to six foot-wide channel, surges to the top of the gorge's north wall. There the white river splits around the rock knobs on top of the ravine, and four falls—one small and three large—spill over the side. The three large cataracts are eight-to-ten-foot thick buttresses of glistening white water. When they crash in the gorge—30 feet deep here but barely 10 feet wide at its narrowest point—they turn the entire canyon into a frothy cauldron and send diaphanous clouds of mist more than 50 feet above the rim.

The falls are like a giant natural humidifier. They make the fence on the rim so wet that water actually drips from its log rails. They also moisten the thick, luxurious carpet of moss on the south wall of the gorge.

If the sun is out, you'll see rainbows here. Where the sun shines on the wet gorge, it makes the rock glisten bright white; in contrast, the ledge in shadow looks almost black. When the sun shines on the dark-green moss, it transforms it into a brilliant yellow-green. When it suffuses the mist with light, the mist becomes opaque, and it hides both the gorge and the bridge.

After you've enjoyed the falls, follow the path downstream, past the bridge, and up to a rise above the river. Here you'll have an upstream view of Sol Duc Falls and the river surging through the long gorge below.

Then you'll quickly come to a trail junction. Follow the Lovers Lane Trail to the right and you'll immediately come to a bluff, where you'll have another view of the river, more than 50 feet below. Then you'll have two more upstream views. By that

Sol Duc Falls (Walk No. 19) crashes into a narrow gorge in the Sol Duc River, sending sprays of mist more than 50 feet above the rim. ▶

point you'll have walked far enough downstream to see rapids, cascades, and light-green pools below the gorge. You'll also see a small, fast creek pouring into the other side of the river. And don't overlook the unusual profusion of bunchberry along the trail; its bright white flowers bloom in late June and early July.

About .2 miles from the falls you'll have yet another bird's-eye view of the cascading river. Then you'll cross a little creek on stones and, soon after, come to Canyon Creek, a major tributary of the Sol Duc. Upstream from the large wooden bridge over the creek you'll see a mass of white cascades, about 8 feet wide and 20 feet long.

From here the Lovers Lane Trail gradually descends to the Sol Duc, where you'll have another view of the river. At that point, however, the Sol Duc is nearly level, with lots of rapids but no big cascades. The trail then moves away from the river, through a mostly unremarkable woods, and it has no more views of the Sol Duc until it reaches the hot springs. So we suggest you turn around either at the Canyon Creek bridge (about .3 miles from the falls) or when you can last see the river (about .4 miles from the bridge) and head back to your car.

20 Pioneer Path

This very easy .3-mile loop follows a level, well-groomed trail through an attractive second-growth hemlock forest. Highly informative signs along the way describe how home-steaders, lumbermen, railroaders, and other early residents of the Olympics exploited the resources of the Sol Duc Valley.

The Walk is at Klahowya Campground, in the Olympic National Forest. To reach the trailhead, take Route 101 to the campground, which is on the north side of the road, about 9.6 miles west of Lake Crescent, 7.4 miles east of the junction of routes 101 and 113, and 18.4 miles northwest of Forks. Turn onto the campground road and, about .2 miles from the highway, turn left onto a one-way loop road. In another .4 miles or so you'll come to the trailhead, which is on the right, between camp-sites 45 and 46. There's a small parking area and a sign explaining that the path was once part of the L. H. Sawyer Homestead, "settled in 1897."

The very smooth, wheelchair-accessible gravel path loops counterclockwise through an open, hemlock woodland, past neat carpets of sorrel, drifts of fern and Oregon grape, and large moss-covered logs. Signs explain how loggers, miners, homesteaders, and railroaders exploited the resources of the Sol Duc Valley: "Pioneers carved homesteads and continually cleared away vegeta-tion for pastures and gardens. Lumberjacks used steel whip saws and lots of muscle to fell trees for lumber and to clear fields. Railroads were built to haul the giant logs to nearby mills."

According to one sign, most homesteaders lived in cabins built of "logs caulked with moss." It was "not unusual for a 12 by 16 foot, one-room cabin to shelter a family of eight."

Another sign explains that the 36-mile Spruce Railroad (see Honorable Mention No. 2) was built during World War I to carry Sitka spruce from the Sol Duc Valley to sawmills in Port Angeles. The "strong but lightweight" spruce was needed to build frames for military airplanes. The railroad did little for the war effort because it wasn't finished until 19 days after the fighting ended, but it did carry logs for a private timber company until after World War II.

Still another sign describes "high stumping." Lumberjacks would cut narrow holes or slots in a large tree, insert springboards into the holes, and stand on the narrow boards so they could cut the tree a couple of yards above the ground, where the tree was narrower, and therefore easier to cut. "Imagine the teamwork and skills needed for two persons to stand on narrow boards several feet above the ground while sawing back and forth through a five-foot diameter tree." To the left of the sign is a ten-foot-high stump with springboard notches cut by lumbermen decades ago.

About halfway around the loop, you'll have a view of the wide, shallow Sol Duc River flowing noisily over its stony bed.

PACIFIC COAST

Great Walks Nos. 21-36 and **Honorable Mention No. 3** are all along the peninsula's unspoiled Pacific Coast.

Northwest Coast

Walk No. 21 (Cape Flattery) and **Honorable Mention No. 3 (Shi Shi Beach),** which offer dramatic ocean views, both begin on the Makah Indian Reservation, which is on the northwesternmost point of the continental United States.

Accommodations include motels and restaurants in Clallam Bay and Sekiu (see below); the Clallam Bay-Sekiu Chamber of Commerce (PO Box 355, Clallam Bay, WA 98326; 360-963-2339) can send you a list. You can buy picnic supplies at Washburn's store in Neah Bay, the principal town on the Makah Reservation.

To reach the trailheads, take Route 112 to Neah Bay.

* * *

If you're driving from Port Angeles or any place east of it, the quickest and most scenic route is to follow Route 112 for its entire length. The eastern end of the road intersects Route 101 about five miles west of downtown Port Angeles.

You'll follow Route 112 for just a few miles before views of Olympic foothills appear on your left. In another 20 miles you'll have a high view across the Strait of Juan de Fuca to Vancouver Island, in British Columbia, almost 20 miles away. Then the road quickly descends to the coast and follows it closely for almost ten miles; along the way you'll have occasional views of the strait, sometimes through trees, on your right.

After passing through Merrill & Ring company timberlands, Route 112 follows the Pysht (pronounced *Piesht*) River upstream, intersects Route 113, and heads north to the seacoast town of **Clallam Bay,** which is located on the two-mile-long cove of the same name.

From there the road goes west, curving along the shore of Clallam Bay. Now you'll have continuous views of the Strait of Juan de Fuca; Sekiu Point, at the western end of the bay; and Slip Point and the Coast Guard station, at the eastern end.

About two miles east of the town of Clallam Bay you'll come to the seaside village of **Sekiu,** which has several motels. The best restaurant on the Northwest Coast is probably the informal and modestly priced **Bayshore Inn,** about halfway between Clallam Bay and Sekiu; its wide-open vista of the bay is one of the best ocean views of any restaurant on the Olympic Peninsula.

About four miles from Clallam Bay (and about 54 miles from Port Angeles) you'll pass the northern end of the **Hoko-Ozette Road,** which goes to Lake Ozette (page 144) and Walks No. 22 and 23.

Then the road curves back to the coast, and for the next ten miles you'll have frequent views of the Strait of Juan de Fuca and Vancouver Island. The road hugs the shore as it winds slowly around bays and over headlands, providing close and often dramatic vistas of rocky beaches, cliffs, and sea stacks. This stretch of highway has the best ocean views of any road on the Olympic Peninsula.

About 12.1 miles from the Hoko-Ozette Road you'll enter the Makah Reservation, and in another three miles you'll come to **Neah Bay**, the reservation's largest community.

About 15.2 miles from the Hoko-Ozette Road you'll reach the **Makah Cultural and Research Center** (360-645-2711), on the left, opposite the Coast Guard Station. One of the best anthropological museums in the Northwest, the center has an outstanding collection of ancient tribal artifacts that were unearthed at an excavation at Cape Alava (Walk No. 22) in the 1970s. The museum is open daily from June 1 to September 15, Wednesday through Sunday the rest of the year.

About .5 miles after the museum, on the left, is Washburn's, a well-stocked general store where you can buy picnic supplies, coffee, pastries, and other goodies.

There are no street or road signs in Neah Bay, so directions must be slightly inexact. To reach the trailheads, keep following Route 112 along the edge of the bay. About 1.4 miles past the museum, follow the road as it curves to the left, away from the ocean; you'll immediately pass a couple of roads entering on the right, then you'll go by the Indian Health Center, on the right, and a dark-brown Presbyterian church, on the left. About 1.5 miles from the museum you'll make a right at the Health Center. In another .1 miles take the second left after the Health Center; there's a black-and-white mileage sign on a tree by the intersection.

Now you'll follow Arrowhead Road to the lush, level flood plain of the slow-moving Waatch River, on your left. On your right you'll see an old quarry and the Makah Tribal Center, which was an Air Force station until 1988.

About four miles from the Makah Museum you'll pass the gravel Hobuck Beach Road, on the left. That road crosses the Waatch River and goes to Hobuck and Sooes beaches, the Makah Nation Fish Hatchery, and the trail to **Shi Shi Beach** *(Honorable Mention No. 3)*. See page 325 for directions to the trailhead.

To get to the Cape Flattery trail (Walk No. 21) keep going straight. About .7 miles past the Hobuck Beach Road, the road to Cape Flattery becomes gravel. In another 2.7 miles you'll pass an old quarry, on the right. On the opposite side of the road, trees have been cut so you can see the Point of Arches on Shi Shi Beach.

About 7.7 miles from the museum you'll come to a road on the left that goes immediately into the parking area at the **Cape Flattery** trailhead. The trail itself begins near the far end of the parking area, on the left.

* * *

If you're driving to Cape Flattery from the south, take Route 101 to Sappho, then Route 113 north to 112.

About 2.1 miles north of Sappho, on the east side

*The red-and-white lighthouse and 50-foot cliffs on Tatoosh Island, off **Cape Flattery** (Walk No. 21), the northwesternmost tip of the continental United States.* ▶

of Route 113, is a collection of lovely cascades known as **Beaver Falls**.

As you approach the falls from the south, the road curves to the right (east) and crosses Beaver Creek. Park on the gravel turnout on the north side of the bridge. You'll glimpse the falls through the trees on the east side of the parking area.

Follow the path to the left of the guardrail. After about 60 feet, the rough trail starts dropping down the steep bank. The best view of the falls is about 50 feet from the road.

The falls are created by a ledge, about 25 feet high and 100 feet wide, that stretches across the creek like a dam. The creek flows over the ledge in a row of cascades. The most exciting cascade is on the left. It tumbles over the ledge, partly sliding down, partly falling over the rock. About halfway down the ledge it shatters against a buttresslike protrusion, becoming a delicate white cone of water that spreads over the rock before falling into the 25-foot-wide pool at the base of the ledge. The white shower of water against the dark ledge is a mesmerizing natural fountain.

A smaller fall to the right merely trickles down the ledge, while another cascade starts sliding down a gentle incline of the ledge but then shoots about 20 feet, almost in a true fall, down to the pool below.

After you've enjoyed the water show, follow the path back to your car.

21 Cape Flattery

This undemanding 1.2-mile round trip takes you to the most dramatic coastline on the Olympic Peninsula. From handsome wooden observation decks you'll see the lighthouse on Tatoosh Island; beautiful green coves ringed by massive 40-foot-high cliffs; surf crashing against monumental buttressed headlands; and ducks, puffins, sea otters, whales, and other fascinating ocean creatures.

The Walk is at the very northwesternmost point of the continental United States. For directions to the trailhead see pages 133-138.

At first the Walk follows an old road that makes a straight but gentle descent into a second-growth forest. You'll barely start walking before you hear the fog horn on Tatoosh Island and sometimes even the cries of seagulls.

At the bottom of the slope, a path splits off to the right. Stay on the road, which goes to the left.

About .2 miles from the parking area, the road becomes a path, which very gradually descends to the ocean through an open forest of cedar, hemlock, and luxurious growths of salal. Much of the way you'll walk on a sturdy cedar boardwalk, interspersed with a few steps, which takes you comfortably over roots and wet spots in the trail.

After about .5 miles, the boardwalk splits. Follow the walkway to the left, which immediately brings you to a handsome rustic wooden deck with cedar log railings and comfortable benches. The deck is on the edge of a bluff that rises 50 feet above a beautiful green, cliff-walled cove that's almost 1,000 feet long and 500 feet wide. On the opposite side of the cove, four sheer headlands jut into the inlet like the prows of giant ships. The near-vertical sides of the cliffs are bare, but their nearly level tops are thickly coated with mosses, salal, and evergreen trees. Look at the bottom of the innermost headlands and, especially at low tide, you'll see caves at the water's edge. In the mouth of the bay are two massive, blocky sea stacks that look like caissons. Like the headlands, the rock islets are covered with a thick evergreen mantle; the verdure drapes over their edges and down their sheer upper sides. Seagulls yelp as they swoop up and down and in and out of the bay; their soft, light, delicate shapes are a splendid contrast with the massive hard, gray cliffs that will be here thousands of years after the gulls flying in front of them have perished. This bay is one of the loveliest seascapes on the Olympic Peninsula. The first time we saw it we were stunned.

After you've given this view the attention it deserves, walk back to the intersection and keep following the boardwalk toward the sea. In a couple of hundred feet you'll come to another wooden deck perched above another green cliffbound cove, to the right of the path. This inlet is a couple

---

Clouds rise like plumes over a giant sea stack and massive headlands at **Cape Flattery** *(Walk No. 21).* ▶

of hundred feet long and about 150 feet wide. On the opposite side of the cove are smooth, massive cliffs, about 60 feet high, with enormous round, buttresslike bases that are interrupted, like an arcade, by large, deep, cavelike arches carved by the sea. One of the largest cave arches has been hollowed out of the 50-foot-high cliff directly in front of the deck and barely 50 feet away. It's at least 15 feet wide and 15 feet deep and soars 40 feet high. It's framed on the left by an awesome buttressed column that at low tide is more than 25 feet across; it looks like the bottom of a giant hoof. On top of the cave, another layer of rock hangs over it like a gigantic hood. The cliffs are awesome, even forbidding, in their monumentality. They resemble an artist's fantasy of the ruin of an enormous temple or the massive fortress of an ancient civilization.

The waves in the little bay smash against the massive escarpment, and cormorants and other sea birds dart in and out of nests in the rock walls. In the distance, beyond the mouth of the cove, you can see the mountains on Vancouver Island.

After you've enjoyed the view, keep following the boardwalk toward the ocean, through sweeps of deep green salal. You'll pass two picnic tables, on the right, surrounded by nothing but a solid sweep of salal. Then you'll come to another wooden deck on the edge of the cliff to your left. From there you have a bird's-eye view of a long, narrow inlet and a pair of deep, tunnel-like 20-foot-high clefts at the bottom of 50-foot-high cliffs. In the distance is the cove you saw from the first deck. Just offshore, seagulls alight on jagged sea stacks.

The trail ends at a large wooden deck at the end of a point at the very tip of Cape Flattery. The view from here may be the most dramatic ocean vista on the Olympic Peninsula.

Straight ahead and barely a mile away is Tatoosh Island, a sturdy-looking quarter-mile-long islet bound by 50-foot-high cliffs with sea caves in the bottom. Perched on its rolling green top is the white-walled, red-roofed Tatoosh Island Lighthouse. To the right of the lighthouse are ruins of bunkers built in World War II. Off the north (right) side of the island (whose name means "thunderbird" in Makah) is a large, low rock where tawny sea lions sprawl in the sun. In front of the island, swarms of seagulls dart incessantly back and forth.

Almost directly below you, near the base of 60-foot cliffs, ducks and puffins bob in the swells and dive for food. Sometimes you'll spot a sea otter swimming on his back, and sometimes even whales, the largest mammals you'll see in the Olympics. The last time we were here—a sunny, breezy day in late July—a shiny black California gray whale surfaced every few seconds as it swam north.

To the left of the point you can see the mouth of the bay you saw at the first overlook, as well as large, blocky sea stacks offshore and waves crashing against the prows of the headlands. To the right of the point, you can see still more cliffs and, more than 20 miles away, the mountains on Vancouver Island, their summits often ringed by white clouds.

On the ground to the right of the deck is an overlook framed by a log railing. From there you can see two enormous cavelike clefts in the rock wall of Cape Flattery; the closest is 30 feet high at low tide and about 10 feet wide. Between the arches of the caves are enormous buttresses that flatten out and look like ancient stone quays extending far into the ocean; the largest is more than 100 feet long; dozens of seagulls rest on their nearly flat surfaces. Although the buttresses have been eroded by the sea, they look so heavy and so massive that, ironically, they seem indestructible, the very essence of permanence. The buttresses are to the headlands as a base is to a classical column or a footing to a building; their great mass only enhances the cliffs rising above them. And like the bases on a column, the monumental headlands at the tip of Cape Flattery are fitting architecture for this special place: the very corner of the continental United States.

The views from this deck are like the views from no other deck in Washington. Can you think of a better place for a long lunch before following the path back to your car?

Lake Ozette

Walks No. 22 and 23 (Cape Alava and Sand Point) both follow cedar boardwalks through the woods to ocean beaches, and both begin at a trailhead at the northern end of Lake Ozette, on the northwestern tip of Olympic National Park.

To reach the trailhead take Route 112 to the

Hoko-Ozette Road, which is about two miles west of Sekiu and four miles west of Clallam Bay. (For a description of the roads to Clallam Bay from both the south and east, see pages 133-134 and 136-138.)

The Hoko-Ozette Road passes roadside clearcuts and curves up the Hoko River Valley for about seven miles before following the Big River Valley almost all the way to Lake Ozette.

About 19.3 miles from Route 112 you'll enter the national park and glimpse Lake Ozette through the trees on your left.

In another 1.9 miles you'll pass **The Lost Resort,** a store, coffee shop, and campground on the right. The store sells basic groceries and camping supplies; the coffee shop serves pizza, sandwiches, and microbrews; the campground has tent and RV sites (but no hookups).

About .4 miles farther you'll pass the **Ozette Campground,** then the **Ozette Ranger Station,** both on the left. The road ends at a parking area just beyond the ranger station. Both Walks begin at the southern end of the parking area. The trail is marked by the same symbol that marks trails on the beaches: a circle divided into quarters, two red and two black, that resembles the BMW logo.

Two warnings:

▶ The boardwalks leading to the beach can be slippery, especially in wet weather. Soft-soled shoes provide better traction than Vibram-soled hiking boots.

▶ Raccoons near the beach are not shy. They'll steal your lunch if you leave your pack unattended.

The Park Service warns you not to feed them or any other wild animal; handouts reinforce both their appetite for human food and their willingness to go after it.

22 Cape Alava

On this moderate 9.6-mile round trip, you'll follow a boardwalk 3.3 miles through the woods to Cape Alava. Then you'll follow the beach to the Wedding Rocks, a celebrated collection of Indian petroglyphs; after that you'll walk to Tskawahyah, or "Cannonball," Island, named for the round rocks scattered at its base. Along the way you'll see the Makah's Osett Memorial, and you'll have views of Ozette Island, Sand Point, the Point of Arches, Tatoosh Island, and other coastal landmarks.

Like Walk No. 23 (Sand Point), this one begins at the Ozette Ranger Station, at the northern end of Lake Ozette. (See pages 144-145 for directions to the trailhead.)

You barely start walking before you cross Coal Creek on a pleasing arch bridge. The stream is named for its charcoal-black water. It flows into the Ozette River (which you'll cross shortly), but it flows so slowly that you usually can't see it moving.

The trail then passes the ranger station, on the left, and a cluster of interesting signs, on the right, that describe the wildlife and other features of this part of the coast. Then you cross the Ozette River on another graceful arch bridge from which you can look up and down the languid 50-foot-wide stream that drains Lake Ozette and flows northwest to the Pacific.

The wide gravelly path then climbs gently through an evergreen forest and forks about .1 miles from the river. The left-hand trail goes to Sand Point, the right-hand path to Cape Alava.

Like the trail to Sand Point, the Cape Alava Trail runs through moist woods with lots of ferns, salal, and evergreen huckleberry. Unlike the largely level Sand Point Trail, however, this route is more rolling. It descends into the valleys of several tiny, sluggish creeks, crosses them on wooden bridges, then climbs out of the hollows, often on wooden stairs. Unlike the Sand Point boardwalk, which is more sloping, much of the Cape Alava boardwalk consists of level stretches interrupted by steps. A level boardwalk is safer than a sloping one, but the endless steps are annoying. They're the main reason this trail isn't as pleasant as the Sand Point Walk.

About halfway to the ocean, you'll come to one of the largest trees on the trail: a giant cedar about seven feet wide at its base. On the other side of the path is a 12-foot-long bench with another, smaller bench behind it. It's a fine resting place if you need it.

Shortly after the halfway point you cross Ahlstrom's Prairie, a nearly treeless savannah named after Lars Ahlstrom, a Swedish settler who pastured his cattle here until 1958. The .5-mile-long prairie is thick with tall grasses, ferns, Labrador tea, and other plants that like moist soil. The boardwalk through the prairie is old and many of its boards are loose, so it rattles loudly (but not unpleasantly) when you walk over it. (Boardwalks running through the woods rattle less, partly because they're often saturated with water, so they swell up tight against their nails, which hold the boards firmly against the joists. The boardwalk in the sunny prairie is often dry—particularly in the summer—so the boards shrink a bit, leaving more space around the nails; as a result, the boards are looser.)

The path reenters the woods near the western end of the prairie and passes a tiny clearing, on the right, with another 12-foot-long bench. The clearing is ringed by tall, lush salal with evergreen trees behind it.

Then the trail crosses a bridge over another prairie, goes into the woods again, and begins its long, gradual descent to the coast. Near the beach you'll walk through an open but shady forest of large Sitka spruces, skunk cabbage, and ferns.

The boardwalk ends near the top of a bluff above the ocean. Then the path curves to the right, passes clusters of sword ferns, and traverses a grassy slope as it gently drops to the beach. Along the way you'll have continuous aerial views of the ocean on your left. (Make sure you don't brush up against the stinging nettles to the left of the path.)

---

*A male black-tailed deer beside massive driftwood at **Cape Alava** (Walk No. 22) Ozette Island is on the left.* ▶

At the tiny meadow at the bottom of the slope, you'll see a trail marker (a circle divided into four quarters) and a sign saying that Sand Point is three miles to the south (left as you face the ocean). See if you can spot people on the top of the tall sea stack at the end of Sand Point and the tooth-shaped sea stack nearby. Directly offshore is the low, tree-covered Ozette Island. The half-mile-long island, with a V-shaped notch in the middle, is only 1,000 yards away. The Bodelteh Islands are just off the coast, about 1.3 miles to the northwest.

Now walk along the beach to the south, toward the Wedding Rocks. Unfortunately, much of the walkway between Cape Alava and Sand Point is a narrow, often pebbly corridor between piles of driftwood near the shore and fields of rocks closer to the sea. You may even have to clamber over a driftwood log or two. So your walk will be neither quick nor effortless. However, it's only a mile to the Wedding Rocks, and if you proceed at a comfortable pace the walk is not unpleasant. As with all ocean walks, do it at the lowest possible tide. And resist the temptation to avoid the beach by following the rough path in the tall grass north of the trail sign. The path quickly peters out and, worse, it's lined with stinging nettles.

At low tide, the ocean here is prickly with countless small rocks sticking out of the water. If the water is unusually calm—just before the tide changes, for instance—the sea resembles a small lake, or even a Japanese stone garden, dotted with hundreds of tiny rock islets. Some parts of the beach are lined with so many small, rounded rocks that it seems to be paved with cobblestones.

Black-tailed deer are also common on this and other ocean beaches, such as Rialto (Walk No. 24), and they're almost tame. Some of them will walk to within ten feet of you before heading away. We saw two bucks lying beside some driftwood logs the last time we were here, and we photographed them from less than 15 feet away. They kept an eye on us, but they seemed unaroused by our presence. We also saw a bald eagle fly overhead with a fish in its talons and raccoons rummaging amid the driftwood.

As you approach the small headland beside the Wedding Rocks you'll see a circular sign, on the left, that marks the northern end of the rough trail that climbs over the point. (It's partially hidden by an enormous upended stump with salal growing on it.) Most of the petroglyphs are in the jumble of rocks about 200 feet south of the sign.

On the flat face of a large rock about ten feet from the spruces on the headland is the couple for whom the Wedding Rocks are named: the famous outline of two people with several bisected oval shapes thought to be fertility symbols. On another rock about 25 feet to the right is a figure of a sailing ship, possibly one seen offshore by the Makah centuries ago; off the bow of the ship is another bisected oval. On still another rock, about 20 feet to the left of the rock with the couple, is a picture of an animal—perhaps a wolf or a dog—with a large head and small stick legs. Beside the animal is another, smaller figure we couldn't identify. On another side of the rock are etchings of what might be fish;

two of them have the bisected oval "fertility" shape. Smaller, less elaborate carvings are nearby.

Some of the figures are of dubious authorship. Real petroglyphs are carved into the rock. On a stone about eight feet to the left of the rock with the two famous figures, what looks like a dollar sign—an S with three (not two) vertical lines through it—is merely *drawn* on the rock, not carved into it. The peace symbol on a large rock beside the ship was probably not executed by a Makah—at least not before the 20th century—and the profile of a face beside it looks authentic, but it too is merely drawn, not carved. Beware of imitations. And beware of adding your own—it's against the law.

Two of the best petroglyphs—the well-known depictions of what appear to be two whales—are a couple of hundred feet farther up the beach, on a rock about 50 feet from the southern end of the trail over the headland.

No one, not even the Makah, knows what the drawings stand for or why they were carved. According to Kirk Wachendorf of the Makah Museum, members of the tribe who might have known about the petroglyphs perished when smallpox and other Caucasian-borne diseases wiped out many Indians in the 19th century.

After you've looked at the etchings, walk back to the Cape Alava Trail. If you'd like some aerial views of the ocean, take the trail over the headland. It's

*These Indian petroglyphs are among more than a dozen found at **Cape Alava** (Walk No. 22). Two of the figures probably represent whales; no one knows what the others symbolize.* ▶

steep and a bit rough and rooty in places, but it's barely a couple of hundred yards long, it takes you along the base of steep cliffs, and it offers some fine vistas from as high as 60 feet above the ocean.

When you get back to the Cape Alava Trail, you have three choices: (1) if you're short of time, you can follow the trail back to your car; (2) if you want to explore the northern part of the cape, you can keep following the beach to the north for another .5 miles; or (3) if the beach is too rough for your taste, you can follow a smooth, level path just off the beach for much of the way.

The path begins in the meadow beside the beach where the Cape Alava Trail ends. Walk northward across the meadow and you'll immediately cross a little creek on a wooden bridge. The trail passes an outhouse, then curves through a level field of tall grass. You'll pass several shaded campsites beside the beach, and you'll have continuing views of Ozette Island through the trees.

About .3 miles north of the creek the trail enters the Ozette Indian Reservation, bends to the left, and takes you back to the beach.

As you walk north on the beach, you'll have better and better views of Tskawahyah Island, a mesa-like sea stack about as tall as it is wide, with evergreen trees growing on its flat top.

Soon you'll pass another, small sea stack, to the left of Tskawahyah Island, that looks roughly like a human head. On the bank to your right is the Makah Ozette Ranger Station (usually unoccupied) and, just beyond it, the Osett Memorial. Built to resemble a traditional Makah building, the memorial is a simple, rustic hut made of cedar planks covered with rough cedar boards that overlap like giant clapboards. A metal plaque inside the building explains that it memorializes the Makah village (Osett) that once stood here. The centuries-old artifacts discovered here in the 1970s form the core of the collection of the Makah Cultural and Research Center, described on page 135.

The 12-by-18-foot hut contains whalebones and a laminated copy of an eloquent and fascinating article in the October 1991 *National Geographic* on Makah whale-hunting customs. The metal plaque says: "Generation to generation our people have shared the wealth from the land and the sea. From this site we have gained appreciation of the wisdom of our forefathers.... in their honor we dedicate this memorial."

If the tide is low enough, you can walk to Tskawahyah Island on a very short sand spit that, in low water, connects the sea stack to the mainland. A sign at the base of the stack tells you that Tskawahyah is "a sacred ground of the Makah Indians" and asks you not to "climb the sides of the island."

Start walking counterclockwise around the island and you'll immediately see why it's nicknamed Cannonball. Below the northeast slope of the island are lots of dark, roundish rocks, one to two feet across, that really do look like giant cannonballs. Some even have a shallow inch-wide hole that resembles the opening in a cannonball where explosives might be inserted. (It also looks like a finger hole in a bowling ball.) Some of the "cannonballs" are split apart; other, dome-shaped rocks look like balls that are somehow emerging from the ledge below them. Most of the full, round cannonball-like stones lie in an area about 100 feet square.

If the tide is low enough, keep walking counterclockwise around the north side of Tskawahyah, and you'll see shallow caves and 50-foot-high cliffs. From this point you'll also have a sweeping view to the north. From right to left, you can see the long row of jagged sea stacks off the Point of Arches on Shi Shi Beach (Honorable Mention No. 3), about five miles away; Archawat and Bahokus peaks on the Makah Reservation; the lighthouse on Tatoosh Island, off Cape Flattery (Walk No. 21); and the mountains of Vancouver Island across the Strait of Juan de Fuca.

When you can't go any farther around the island without getting wet, walk back to the Cape Alava Trail and follow it back to your car. (And make sure you return before a rising tide covers the spit, or you *will* get wet.) You can follow the beach all the way back to the Cape Alava Trail; or, if you tire of walking the stony strand, you can walk through one of the campsites on the left, pick up the path just off the beach, and follow it back to the trail.

23 Sand Point

*A walker on the beach just south of **Sand Point** (Walk No. 23), one of the largest, smoothest beaches on the Olympic Peninsula.* ▶

On this moderate round trip—as short as seven miles or as long as nine, depending on how far you want to walk along the beach—you follow a comfortable boardwalk three miles through the woods to Sand Point. There you climb a 40-foot-high sea stack for panoramic ocean views and stroll along one of the largest, smoothest beaches on the Olympic Peninsula.

Like Walk No. 22 (Cape Alava), this one begins at the ranger station at the northern tip of Lake Ozette and follows the route of Walk No. 22 for the first 800 feet or so. See pages 146-147 for a trail description.

When the trail splits about .1 miles after the bridge over the Ozette River, take the path to the left, which goes to Sand Point. (The right-hand trail goes to Cape Alava.)

You'll immediately begin walking on a two-foot-wide cedar boardwalk through a moist, dense second-growth forest thick with salal, deer ferns, and evergreen huckleberry. Much of this forest was burned in the past, and you can still see fire-blackened snags. A lot of the boardwalk is so old that it actually resembles a dirt path, for several reasons: It has sunk into the forest floor, so the top of the planking is often at ground level; moss grows on the ends of the boards (where feet are not apt to crush it) just as it would grow on the edge of a dirt path; and some of the planks have turned so dark that they're almost the color of a dirt path. They look dark partly because old wood tends to absorb more water and retain it longer than new wood, and wet boards look darker than dry ones. The smooth, firm, often nearly level boardwalk makes walking so easy that the three miles to the beach pass quickly.

As you get closer to the shore you'll start hearing the surf, and you'll glimpse the ocean through the open woods. You'll pass a giant Sitka spruce, on the right, that's six feet thick at chest height and 14 feet wide near the bottom of its buttresslike root spread.

The boardwalk ends beside campsites next to a stony beach. Walk to the edge of the beach and you'll get your first view of the low, grassy Sand Point, on the left, and the sandy, 40-foot-tall sea stack at the end of it that you'll climb in a few minutes. In the surf to the right of the point are a half-dozen sea stacks, three with evergreen trees growing on their flat tops. At low tide, the narrow bay is dotted with countless dark brown rocks.

Return to the main trail and follow it through a pretty Sitka spruce forest and luxurious chest-high sweeps of salal. Less than .1 mile ahead the path is covered by another, short boardwalk; near the middle of it is a sign indicating that there's a privy on the path to the right.

Follow the right-hand path. You'll pass more campsites, on both sides of the trail, then the privy, on the right, in a couple of hundred feet. Immediately after the outhouse you'll come to the beach. Follow the beach to the left and, in another couple of hundred feet, you'll reach the base of the sea stack at the end of the point.

Climb the steep but short (100-foot-long) path to

the top of the stack. When you get there you may be startled by how small the top is—it's about the size of a large room. The stack slopes rather gently to the north, south, and east but drops precipitously toward the ocean. The sea, of course, is gradually eroding the stack away, and one day it'll disappear. Now, however, the thick grass on its smooth, flat summit is a perfect spot for picnicking, lounging, and savoring its unusual 360-degree view.

To the north you can see as far as Ozette Island, the Bodelteh Islands, and the Flattery Rocks off Cape Alava, more than three miles away. On a clear day you can see as far south as Cape Johnson, more than 18 miles away. You can also see how different the north side of Sand Point is from the south. The north beach is narrow, and the entire bay is studded with rocks. The south beach, in contrast, is a vast crescent of flat, smooth, almost level sand. More than a mile long and several hundred feet wide at low tide, the beach is one of the largest strands on the Olympic Peninsula. Even its wide, shallow surf is virtually unbroken by rocks.

After you've enjoyed the view, climb down from the stack and walk south on the beach. You'll immediately pass another sea stack, about 18 feet high and about 40 feet at its widest point. Like most stacks, this one is all rock (no sand).

You'll quickly discover that the beach is a perfect walking surface: smooth and as firm as the boardwalk you walked on earlier, so firm that your shoes will barely leave a print in the sand.

About .1 miles north of Sand Point you'll come to Wish Creek, a modest streamlet just two to three inches deep as it burbles across the beach. If you want to cross it without getting your feet wet, traverse it on rocks or logs farther upstream.

You'll cross another tiny creek in another .5 miles or so, and if you look to your left you'll see the red-and-black circle marking the trail to Ericsons Bay on Lake Ozette (a part of the lake accessible only by boat or by this trail).

In another .6 miles you'll come to tide pools where you'll see sea anemones and starfish; take care not to step on them.

About .5 miles later you'll approach the headlands to the north of the Yellow Banks. You can round these points at low tide; at higher tides you'll have to walk through a narrow tunnel in the rock (be sure to return before the tide blocks the tunnel as well).

Walk as little or as much of the beach as you like, then retrace your steps to your car.

LaPush Area Beaches

Walks No. 24-27, which take you along four scenic Pacific beaches, all begin in or near the seaside village of LaPush. The principal settlement on the Quileute Indian Reservation, LaPush is at the mouth of the Quillayute River, about 14 miles west of the town of Forks.

To reach the trailheads, take Route 101 to the

LaPush Road, which is about a mile north of downtown Forks, and follow it toward the coast. About 7.8 miles from Route 101 you come to the **Mora Road**. To reach Walk No. 24 (Rialto Beach) follow the Mora Road (described on page 164) to the coast. To reach Walks No. 25-27 stay on the LaPush Road.

The closest accommodations to Walks No. 25-27 are at the rustic **Ocean Park Resort** on First Beach (Walk No. 25) in LaPush. Owned and managed by the Quileute tribe, the resort offers a wide range of choices: tent sites; RV campsites with three-way hookups; primitive "campers' cabins" with mattresses, hot plates, refrigerators, and wood stoves, but no hot water or showers; motel rooms with kitchens; and more elaborate one- to three-bedroom cabins with kitchens, electric heat, and baths with showers. Most of the latter also have fireplaces or glass-front wood stoves, spacious decks, and some of the best ocean views of any lodging on the Olympic Peninsula. Unfortunately, even the high-end units show some wear and tear, but the beachside location can't be beat. The resort (PO Box 67, LaPush, WA 98350; 800-487-1267, 360-374-5267) is open all year.

Right beside the resort is the year-round **Lonesome Creek Store & Resort** (360-374-4333), which provides basic groceries, snacks, tent sites, teepees, and RV campsites with ocean views and three-way hookups.

Other nearby accommodations are at the **Three Rivers Resort,** which is at the junction of the LaPush and Mora roads, about five miles from Rialto Beach and six miles from LaPush. The year-round resort (7764 LaPush Rd., Forks, WA 98331; 360-374-5300) has housekeeping cabins, RV campsites with two- and three-way hookups, a laundry, showers, and a small restaurant and grocery store.

The largest and least expensive selection of groceries in the area can be found at the Thriftway or the Pay and Save Shop Rite, both in Forks. There are also several motels, private campgrounds, and B&Bs in the area; the Forks Chamber of Commerce (PO Box 1249, Forks, WA 98331; 1-800-443-6757, 360-374-2531) will send you a free list.

24 Rialto Beach

This moderate 4.7-mile round trip may be the most absorbing beach walk on the Olympic Peninsula. You'll walk through a splendid natural sculpture garden comprised of gigantic sea stacks and through the 30-foot-deep natural arch known as the Hole-in-the-Wall. You'll climb a headland with a bird's-eye view of the beach, and you'll walk to the base of Little James Island, where you can see starfish and sea anemones. Along the way you'll also have close views of James Island, Gunsight Rock, Cake Rock, and the Quillayute River estuary.

It's best to take this walk at the lowest possible tide, for two reasons. First, the ledgy floor of the Hole-in-the-Wall is under water during medium and high tides. Second, the southern part of Rialto Beach is narrow and relatively steep, so the smooth, sandy strip near the surf is also covered by high and medium tides. If you want to walk through the Hole-in-the-Wall safely and without getting your feet wet, and if you don't want to walk on rocks or get your feet wet during the beginning of the Walk, take it at the lowest tide possible.

Rialto Beach is on the north side of the Quillayute River, opposite the village of LaPush.

To get to the beach, follow the LaPush Road (see page 161), as far as the Three Rivers Resort, which is about 7.8 miles west of Forks. Then take a right onto the **Mora Road;** almost immediately you'll cross the broad Sol Duc River, which flows into the Quillayute just a few yards downstream.

About 2.7 miles from the LaPush Road you'll enter the national park; shortly after that you'll pass the **Mora Ranger Station and Campground.** The road then runs through a lovely forest of Sitka spruces and other large evergreens.

About 4.2 miles from the LaPush Road you'll cross the dark, slow-moving Dickey River, which flows into the Quillayute a few hundred feet downstream. In another .5 miles the road curves along the north bank of the Quillayute. Here you'll see James Island at the mouth of the river and Little James Island to the right. The flat mud islands in the river, which usually rise just a few inches above the water, are often covered with hundreds of resting seagulls. On

---

*Hikers are silhouetted in the Hole-in-the-Wall, a 30-foot-deep tunnel in a 70-foot-high headland on **Rialto Beach** (Walk No. 24). Beyond the tunnel you can see Little James Island, which is just off **First Beach** (Walk No. 25), in the Quileute Indian village of LaPush.* ▶

the south side of the river is the village of LaPush. A plaque beside the road relates how the Quileute hunted whales and seals from this village for centuries. In another .3 miles the road ends at the Rialto Beach parking area.

The Walk begins at the northern end of the parking lot, near the rest rooms. Follow the paved path through the shaded picnic area, cross the narrow strip of rocks at the end of the path, and you'll be on the beach. From the stony sand you can see James Island and Little James Island to your left, the flat-topped Cake Rock about two miles offshore, a cluster of jagged sea stacks to the right of Cake Rock, and a row of about eight rough, sharp-pointed sea stacks at a headland about 1.5 miles up the beach. The Hole-in-the-Wall is in the stone headland to the right of the sea stacks, closest to shore.

As you head north, toward the stacks, the beach gets wider, smoother, more level, and easier to walk on. As you gradually come abreast of Cake Rock, you'll see that the "cake" appears to lean to the left, as if it was disturbed while it was baking.

About a mile from the parking area you'll come to Ellen Creek, slicing crisply through the sand. If you want to cross it without getting your feet wet, you'll probably have to walk upstream (usually less than 300 feet) until you find some driftwood that someone has usually laid across the water.

As you get closer to the sea stacks you'll notice (at low tide) small rocks in the surf that look like miniature stone islands. They'd be perfect for a Japanese garden.

Less than half a mile beyond Ellen Creek you'll

come to the first of several enormous sea stacks that comprise a natural sculpture garden in front of the Hole-in-the-Wall. The first stack is a massive but graceful piece of sandstone, about 30 feet across and 40 feet high and nicely pointed at the top. To its left is a wide, low piece of rock, about 20 feet across but no more than three feet high, that resembles a Henry Moore sculpture. The smooth, light-colored stone looks like a miniature landscape, with little mountains and valleys, and hollows filled with seawater that look like tiny green lakes. Patches of bright green sea moss add color.

Just ahead and closer to the ocean is what at first looks like an enormous sea stack, about 80 feet tall and 80 feet wide at the base. To the right of the stack, at the bottom of a long rock headland, you can see the Hole-in-the-Wall. Just offshore, the surf is dotted with several dozen small rocks.

As you approach the giant sea stack, you'll see that it's actually two stacks divided by a deep chasm that reaches almost all the way down to the beach. The right-hand stack is about 50 feet thick at its widest point, and its flat, near-vertical walls are almost 80 feet high. The left-hand stack is about 40 feet tall and 25 feet thick. Walk between the stacks and you'll see that the smaller one has an intriguing irregular hole that's about eight feet high, about two feet wide at its widest point, and barely a foot across at its narrowest span, near the middle. Be careful not to step on the starfish and sea anemones on the rocks beneath your feet.

Keep walking toward the Hole-in-the-Wall and you'll have another surprise: Just beyond the split stack is another sea stack, at least as large as the 80-footer, but with a pointed top and sheer walls. The 25-foot-wide passage between the two rocks is an awesome shady canyon.

Beyond the last stack is an enormous, smooth, nearly bare rock headland, almost 70 feet high and 150 feet long, reaching out from the shore. At the bottom of the rock, and close to its left side, is the Hole-in-the-Wall, a gracefully rounded arch about 14 feet wide, 16 feet tall at its highest point, and almost 30 feet deep. To the left of the rock, and separated from it at low tide by a ledgy causeway, is yet another sea stack, about 40 feet high.

If the tide is low enough, walk through the Hole-in-the-Wall. As you approach the tunnel, you'll pass lots of tidepools and rocks teeming with starfish and other sea life.

As you emerge from the northern end of the tunnel, you'll see low rocks and tide pools covering the beach. Look behind you and you'll see that the northern entrance to the Hole-in-the-Wall has a wonderful pointed, if slightly lopsided Gothic shape. Look to the left of the tunnel and you'll see how the sheer rock headland curves to the north, parallel to the narrow beach.

For a dramatic gull's-eye view, take the steep but short path that climbs over the headland. It's marked by the usual sign: a circle divided into four

*At low tide, Little James Island is linked to **Rialto Beach** (Walk No. 24) on a low, narrow sand spit. Breaking waves elegantly echo the beach. The northern end of James Island is on the left. The V-shaped Gunsight Rock is behind Little James Island.* ▶

quarters. (If the tide is too high to walk through the Hole-in-the-Wall, you'll have to take this path to cross the headland.) The narrow path switches back and forth up to the crest of the ridge that links the headland to the shore. Here, about 300 feet from the beach, the path intersects another trail that runs along the crest of the ridge toward the sea. Follow that trail through a thick mat of salal and, about 50 feet from the trail junction, you'll reach an overlook with long views up and down the beach. The Hole-in-the-Wall and the tidepools around it are almost directly below. The massive sea stacks are to your left. Five miles south is the cluster of sea stacks known as the Quillayute Needles. North of the Needles are James and Little James islands and Gunsight Rock. Cake Rock is offshore.

* * *

After you've enjoyed the view, walk back toward the southern end of the beach. But instead of retracing your steps to the parking area, keep following the beach toward Little James Island. About two miles south of the Hole-in-the-Wall and about .5 miles south of the parking area, you'll reach the massive rock jetty that runs parallel to the beach and separates it from the mouth of the Quillayute River. If the tide is low enough, you can keep walking along the beach to the right of the jetty. You can also climb up on the jetty and follow the wide, smooth gravelly path on top of it. If you walk along the jetty, your viewpoint will be loftier, of course, and you'll have continuing panoramic views of both the ocean, on your right, and the Quillayute River estuary, on your left, and closer and closer views of James and Little

James islands and Gunsight Rock. The jetty path gradually gets rougher, however, and you'll soon have to climb over driftwood and dodge holes in the footing. At that point, if the tide is still low enough, you may want to climb back down to the beach.

About .7 miles from the parking area you'll come to a break in the jetty. Here, at low tide, a sand spit connects the jetty to the rocky base of Little James Island, just a couple of hundred feet away. You'll find lots of starfish, sea anemones, and other sea life on its surf-soaked rocks. If you want to avoid wet feet, be sure to walk back to the jetty before the tide covers up the spit.

When you're ready, head back to the parking area, either on the jetty or, if the tide is low enough, on the narrow beach beside it.

25 First Beach

This two-mile round trip is an easy stroll along one of the most picturesque beaches on the Olympic coast—a wide stretch of smooth sand framed by Quateeta Head and the Quillayute Needles on one end and the steep-sided James and Little James islands on the other. You'll have uninterrupted views of all these landmarks, plus a look at Cake Island and Gunsight Rock, and you'll see starfish and sea anemones on the rocks at the south end of the beach.

The Walk begins in the village of LaPush, near the end of the LaPush Road. About .3 miles past the Ocean Park Resort (see page 162), the Lapush Road curves sharply to the right near the Quileute Tribal School (a former Coast Guard station). Park here, walk behind the school buildings, and follow the dirt road that takes you quickly to the northern end of the beach.

On your right you'll see the massive stone jetty that separates the beach from the mouth of the Quillayute River. Off the mouth of the river, barely 500 feet beyond the seaward end of the jetty, is James Island. More than 1,500 feet long, James is the largest near-shore island on the Olympic coast. Its location and its high, clifflike sides once made the island very useful to the Quileutes. When they were attacked by the Makah (who lived farther up the coast—see pages 133-156), they would quickly retreat to the island, which became their natural castle. On top of its formidable walls, surrounded by the moat of the sea, the Quileutes could fend off their enemies.

North of the jetty, on the other side of the river, is Little James Island. A smaller version of its namesake, Little James is just a few hundred feet wide. Its high, flat, steep sides, eroded bare by the sea, and its flat top make it look like a trapezoid, or a gravelly pyramid with its top sliced off and surrealistically covered with spruce trees.

*Sunset on the broad, smooth **First Beach** (Walk No. 25), in the village of LaPush. The steep-sided, spruce-topped James and Little James islands are silhouetted on the horizon.*
▶

Climb up on the jetty and your view will expand. Now you'll see the bottom of both James and Little James islands, including the cavelike hole at the base of Little James. To the right of James is Gunsight Rock, named for its tapering vertical shape and especially the wide V-shaped notch on the top. To the right of Little James and two miles off shore is small, gray Cake Rock, well named for its long, flat top and vertical sides. You'll also have a broad view up and down the Quillayute River, including its low muddy islands, often covered with hundreds of seagulls.

If you feel like walking along the jetty towards James Island, you'll have an even closer view of the Quileute's former redoubt. But be warned: your footing will be a rough bed of rocks, not smooth sand.

When you're ready, turn around and start walking toward the southern end of the beach. Ahead of you will be the point of Quateeta Head, sloping gently into the sea and pointing to the archipelago of off-shore sea stacks known as the Quillayute Needles. Some of the Needles are sharply pointed, just like needles; others are lower and flat-topped. On your left, extending the full length of the beach, is a vast pile of giant trees and logs washed up by the tide. The last time we were there we saw one tree about halfway down the beach that was seven feet thick at the base; the remains of its roots reached ten feet into the air.

First Beach is one of the widest strands on the Olympic coast—so wide that there's always a broad stretch of smooth sand to walk on, even at high tide.

The ocean is so shallow that waves start breaking hundreds of feet offshore, and as many as a dozen breakers at a time roll toward the beach.

The Walk ends at the steep, 80-foot-high cliffs of Quateeta Head. Below the headwall is a cluster of rocks rinsed by the tide. The rocks are covered not only with dark layers of mollusks and barnacles, but also with green sea anemones and brown and orange starfish — be careful not to disturb them. When we were there last, the surf had spread a neat, flat layer of very smooth wet sand between the rocks, making the scene look like a Japanese sand-and-rock garden. It was one of those lovely rare moments when nature creates a garden all by itself.

As you retrace your steps to your car, enjoy the views of the beach, the ocean, and James and Little James islands from another direction.

26 Second Beach

This undemanding 3.6-mile round trip provides continuous views of an exciting collection of headlands, arches, rocks, and sea stacks. En route to the beach you'll walk through a lush coastal rain forest of ferns, salal, and giant evergreen trees.

The Walk begins on the LaPush Road, on the Quileute Reservation, about .7 miles east of the LaPush Ocean Park Resort and about 13.2 miles west of Route 101. Look for the "Second Beach" sign at the west end of an unpaved parking area on the south side of the road.

The .7-mile trail to the beach is wide, smooth, and often level. You barely start walking before you pass a spring on the left that collects water for the Quillayute fish hatchery. Then the trail descends to a small creek, crosses the stream on a wooden bridge, turns sharply to the left, gently climbs up to a small plateau, and enters the national park.

So rich and lush is this damp, shady forest that the woods on both sides of the trail are almost filled with the remains of dead trees—so many logs that, if you left the trail and bushwacked through the woods, your feet would almost never touch ground, just moist, rotting logs. You'll also see giant stumps as wide as small rooms—vestiges of logging done before these woods became part of the national park.

Near the end of the trail you begin to hear the sound of surf. Soon after, the trail switches back and forth down the steep bank above the beach.

As you walk onto the beach you'll enjoy the most impressive view of the Walk. Ahead of you is a semicircle of more than a dozen rocks and sea stacks, both large and small; the surf-carved stone is a natural sculpture garden mounted on a wave-washed beach bounded by massive ledges, Quateeta Head and Teahwhit Head, on each end.

Close to shore are three sea stacks so large that spruce trees grow on top of them. The tallest one, Crying Lady Rock, is as big as a small island. Behind

*Massive sea stacks, including the Quillayute Needles off-shore, are a natural sculpture garden on **Second Beach** (Walk No. 26), just south of the village of LaPush.* ▶

them, about .7 miles offshore, is the cluster of pointed and flat-topped rocks known as the Quillayute Needles. On your right, about .3 miles away, is a natural arch carved by the sea into the base of Quateeta Head.

For a closer look at the arch and the headland, walk to your right. In about .2 miles you'll come to a cluster of rocks near the arch; like many other coastal rocks, these are home to starfish, sea anemones, and other sea life. Be careful not to hurt them.

After you've explored this end of the beach, turn around and head for the other end, more than a mile away. Like First Beach (Walk No. 25), this one is wide and the water is shallow. Waves break far offshore and the surf is usually ribbed with at least half a dozen breakers, all parallel to each other.

You'll cross a creek (on stones and driftwood) where you first came upon the beach. Then, as you pass Crying Lady Rock, you'll notice another large sea stack behind it. Closer to Teahwhit Head you'll see another natural arch, a sail-shaped hole at the bottom of the headland. At low tide, you can see still another, smaller natural arch in one of the sea stacks to the left of Teahwhit Head.

About halfway down the beach you'll cross another creek, and about .5 miles after that you'll come to a small headland. If the tide is low enough, you'll be able to walk around this point without getting your feet wet. If you go beyond this point, you'll cross a third creek and reach another cluster of rocks where you'll see more starfish, anemones, and other sea creatures. You won't be able to see through the sail-shaped arch on Teahwhit Head any more, but you will have better and better views of the smaller arch to the left of it. In fact, at very low tides, you'll be able to walk through it.

Walk as far down the beach as you care to, but if you want to keep your feet dry, remember to return while you still have dry passage around the small headland. As you retrace your route to your car, enjoy the beach's rock-and-water tableau from another perspective.

27 Third Beach

This moderate six-mile round trip brings you to a relatively uncrowded, isolated beach with dramatic views of dozens of sea stacks, striking headlands, and a 50-foot waterfall. En route you'll follow a pleasant 1.6-mile trail through a coastal rain forest.

The Walk begins on the LaPush Road, on the Quileute Indian Reservation, about 2.1 miles east of the LaPush Ocean Park Resort and about 11.5 miles west of Route 101. A sign saying "Third Beach" marks a large unpaved parking area on the south side of the road.

At first the trail to the beach follows an old road— a flat, straight allée through a mixed forest of alders and other young trees. Then the track becomes a wide, smooth, often gravelly trail through an older, more open, mainly evergreen forest. Ancient logs—

the moist, decaying corpses of trees—lie in the woods beside the trail, and a few dark, giant stumps are reminders that these woods were cut for timber before they became part of the national park; the stumps also reveal that the trees cut for lumber were bigger than almost anything growing here now. The path, often level, is fringed with ferns and large drifts of salal. Nearer the beach it's edged with big patches of sorrel, whose clusters of four small heart-shaped leaves make it look a bit like four-leaf clover.

About .2 miles from the ocean, the trail begins its dramatic descent to the beach, switching gently back and forth down the bank of a steep ravine lined with sorrel and ferns. As you descend you have a continuous view of the ocean framed by the V-shaped slopes of the canyon. The last time we were there—a foggy late September day—the smell and smoke of campfires drifted up the ravine and warmed the cool, moist air.

After crossing the creek at the bottom of the ravine (on logs) and traversing the large jam of drift logs at the mouth of the creek, you'll be on Third Beach and at the head of Strawberry Bay, a crescent-shaped inlet bounded on the north by the 200-foot cliffs of Teahwhit Head and on the south by the 300-foot cliffs of Taylor Point. To the left of Taylor Point a wispy waterfall drops more than 50 feet down the bluff above the beach. Straight ahead of you is a thick cluster of sea stacks, many of them in the rock archipelago known as the Giants Graveyard, two miles away.

Third Beach is narrower and steeper than either First Beach or Second Beach, so the water is deeper and the breakers fewer. You're apt to see ducks and cormorants diving for food.

Partly because the beach is enclosed at each end, and partly because it's farther from a trailhead and less crowded than any other beach in the area, it feels both wilder and more isolated.

To explore the northern end of the beach, walk to your right, toward the spruce-topped Teahwhit Head. In about .4 miles you'll come to a group of rocks below a ravine, where you'll see sea anemones and starfish.

For a closer look at the falls and the sculpture of the Giants Graveyard, head south. In about .8 miles you'll pass a cable ladder that leads to the trail that takes long-distance hikers overland, across Taylor Point. In another .2 miles (if the tide is low enough) you'll be at the base of the falls.

When you're ready, turn around and retrace your steps to your car.

Kalaloch Coast

Walks Nos. 28-36 are in the southwest corner of Olympic National Park. Walk No. 33 traverses a coastal rain forest; the others take you to some of the smoothest, sandiest beaches on the Olympic Peninsula. The beaches are also close to trailheads, so they're also among the most accessible in the park. All Walks but one are easy or undemanding.

Walk No. 28 (Oil City Beach), the northernmost Walk in the area, begins at the western end of the Oil City Road (see below).

Walks No. 29-36 all begin on Route 101, which in this part of the peninsula runs very close to the ocean—sometimes so close that you have continuous views of the sea and Destruction Island from your car. In fact, the ocean views from this stretch of Route 101 are rivaled on the peninsula only by the vistas from Route 112 (which takes you to Walk No. 21 and Honorable Mention No. 3).

Another dramatic sight along Route 101 is a gigantic, 20-foot-thick cedar tree located about five miles north of Kalaloch Lodge (see below), .5 miles south of Beach 6 (Walk No. 30), and 1.8 miles north of Beach 4 (Walk No. 31). Look for the sign on the east side of the highway. An unpaved .3-mile road takes you to a parking loop, from which you follow a 50-foot path to the tree. The fluted trunk of the centuries-old Goliath is as wide as a cabin. A plaque explains that coastal Indians used western red cedar to make an astonishing number of things: houses and seagoing canoes, harpoon line from the branches, diapers and bandages from the soft outer bark, clothing, baskets, and mattresses from the inner bark.

Accommodations near the trailheads include **Kalaloch Lodge** and **Kalaloch Campground,** both located on the ocean just north of the park's **Kalaloch Ranger Station,** and **South Beach Campground,** south of Beach 1 (Walk No. 36). There are a half-dozen other campgrounds nearby, including the **Cottonwood Recreation Area** on the Oil City Road.

Situated on a coastal bluff, the attractive brown-shingled **Kalaloch Lodge** has both second-story guest rooms and housekeeping cabins, many with ocean views, plus a small store, a gas station, a coffee shop, and a justly popular dining room serving three meals daily; the dining room also has a fine view of Kalaloch Creek and the ocean beyond it. A national park concession, the lodge (157151 Highway 101, Forks, WA 98331; 360-962-2271) is open year round.

The next-closest lodging is on Lake Quinault (see pages 226-231), which is 32 miles southeast of Kalaloch Lodge, or in Forks, which is 35 miles north. The closest large grocery stores are in Forks.

28 Oil City Beach

This undemanding 2.8-mile round trip follows the Hoh River to a beach with continuous views of North Rock, Middle Rock, Hoh Head, Perkins Reef, Diamond Rock, and other coastal landmarks. You'll also enjoy sweeping vistas of the Hoh.

As you might guess, there's no city anywhere near this beach and no oil either. It got its name in the 1930s, when an oil fever swept the area. Anticipating that 11 newly drilled wells would create a boomtown, realtors started selling lots. Alas, neither the oil nor the "city" materialized. All that's left of Oil City is its name.

The Walk begins at the end of the Oil City Road, just north of the Hoh Indian Reservation. To reach the trailhead, turn off Route 101 onto the Oil City

Road about .5 miles north of the Hoh River Bridge. The junction, which is marked by a sign for the Cottonwood Recreation Area, is about 13 miles south of Forks and about 22 miles north of Kalaloch Lodge.

The road, mostly paved, curves through pleasant woods. About three miles from Route 101 you pass the road to the Cottonwood Recreation Area, on the left. In another seven miles or so, the road narrows slightly and passes a couple of ranches; you may see cattle in pastures along the road. Almost 10.5 miles from Route 101, you enter the national park, and the road, now gravel, soon ends at a small parking area on a bluff above the Hoh River.

The trail to the beach begins beside a signboard at the west end of the parking area. The path crosses tiny creeks on wooden bridges as it curves along the top of the bluff. Through trees on your left you'll catch glimpses of the wide, smooth, blue-green waters of the Hoh and occasional rowboats on the opposite bank, which is the northernmost tip of the Hoh Indian Reservation.

Soon you'll come to a dramatic overlook, at the very edge of the bluff, with a 180-degree vista. You'll be able to look up and down the Hoh, now directly below. On your right, you'll see waves rolling onto the beach and sandbars at the mouth of the river, half a mile away. The sharp-pointed North Rock is two miles offshore.

Then the trail winds down from the bluff, closer to the river, and passes through a thicket of alders and blackberries.

About .8 miles from the parking area the trail

ends at the rocky north bank of the river, which makes a wide curve to the right as it flows to the sea. Follow the riverbank until you reach the narrow mouth of the Hoh, about a mile from the trailhead. Here the river rushes into the sea through a 30-foot-wide channel it has carved through the sand beach. During an outgoing tide, when the ocean is ebbing away from the river, the Hoh surges through this channel at more than 10 miles an hour. On the beach south of the river you sometimes see Indians casting their nets for fish.

Your wide view from the shore includes a half-dozen rock or island landmarks. On your far left is Abbey Island (seen on Walk No. 29), just offshore and 2.7 miles to the south. To the right of Abbey Island and almost four miles away is South Rock. To the right of South Rock and more than five miles away is the long, low Destruction Island. To the right of Destruction Island, and just .7 miles away, is Middle Rock. Look for its outward-sloping upper sides and center notch. Just to the right of Middle Rock but a mile farther away is North Rock. Right of North Rock and 3.5 miles to the northwest are the tiny islets of Perkins Reef. Immediately to the right of the reef and 1.5 miles closer to the beach are the 180-foot cliffs of Hoh Head. In front of the head, and only about .5 miles away from you, are more rocks and shoals, including the well-named sharp-pointed Diamond Rock.

You'll have closer views of Diamond Rock and other landmarks off to your left as you walk the beach to the north. The last time we were here—a sunny, breezy early September afternoon—waves broke on shoals far offshore and, because the weather was clear and bright, the seascape was a study in blues. The sky and the sea far offshore were deep blue. Nearer shore the ocean was aqua and an even greener aqua on the shore side of breaking waves. The water retreating back into the sea after breaking on shore was a rich marine blue flecked with brilliant white. After the wave had gone, the water-soaked beach was a glossy blue, reflecting the hue of the sky.

Less than .5 miles from the mouth of the Hoh, you'll come to two small headlands. To go around them you'll have to walk on stones, even at low tide. This is a good place to turn around and retrace your steps to your car. On the way back to the river you'll have a continuous view of the islands and rocks to the south.

29 Ruby Beach

This round trip takes you to one of the most interesting and exciting beaches in the park. As soon as you reach the shore you'll see waves crashing against Abbey Island and more than a half-dozen sea stacks, some so close you can walk to them at low tide without getting your feet wet. You'll also enjoy continuous long-range views of Destruction Island, South Rock, Hoh Head, Teawhit Head, and other landmarks, and as you approach the beach you'll have splendid bird's-eye vistas of the coast.

This outing can be as short and easy as a .3-mile round trip to the most interesting part of the beach, or as long as a moderate eight-mile round trip up and down the shore.

The Walk begins on Route 101, about 7.9 miles north of Kalaloch Lodge. Turn off the highway at the sign for Ruby Beach and follow a short, .2-mile road to the large parking area. En route you'll have a view of the ocean over the bluff on your left.

The trail to the beach begins at the northern end of the parking area. Just to the right of the trail is a graceful overlook framed by a log-rail fence. From here you can enjoy one of the most memorable coastal views on the Olympic Peninsula. Through an opening in the spruce trees you can see surf crashing against a cluster of sea stacks at the edge of the beach; foamy white water plumes contrast beautifully with the dark-gray rocks. A sign here explains that sea stacks are the remains of headlands that have been eroded away by centuries of pounding waves. Directly behind the sea stacks is the tall, narrow Abbey Island, its flat top crowned with spruce trees; like sea stacks, its bare, straight, almost vertical 60-foot-high walls have been eroded by centuries of waves. To the right of the island and five miles away, the steep cliffs of Hoh Head jut into the ocean. Left of Hoh Head and more than 14 miles in the distance is Teahwhit Head, which separates Second Beach (Walk No. 26) from Third Beach (Walk No. 27), near LaPush. Directly below the overlook and just to the right of the beach is Cedar Creek. Sometimes there's a large, glass-smooth pool near the mouth of the stream; it's created when beach sand, pushed by the surf, forms a dam across the creek. From the overlook, the pool sometimes looks like a graceful arm of the sea, extending into the woods like a little bay.

A smooth, wide 300-foot path descends gently to the beach through open woods. About halfway down you come to a bench at a bend in the trail. Here, through the spruce trees, you have another aerial view: a long vista up and down the beach, which is dotted with large gray rocks constantly drenched by broken white surf.

After you cross the tangle of driftwood at the end of the trail, go to your right and you'll immediately come to the cluster of sea stacks you saw from the overlook at the trailhead. Note the two jagged holes in the first one, through which you can see the sky. These huge pointed rocks make Ruby Beach one of the liveliest, most exciting beaches in the park, not just because they're interesting to look at but also because they give the surf something big to crash against. The waves advance to the shore, one after the other, like ranks of 19th-century infantry crossing a battlefield, only to break against the rocks, sending misty showers of white water high into the air. It's a continuous white-water show that lasts as long as you want to watch it.

Unlike the beaches south of Kalalach Lodge, Ruby Beach is narrow. But if the tide is low enough, you'll be able to walk past the jumble of large point-

---

*At **Ruby Beach** (Walk No. 29), on the Kalaloch Coast, the light of the setting sun glistens on wet rocks and suffuses the mist of waves crashing against massive sea stacks.* ▶

ed rocks near the mouth of Cedar Creek and another pile in the narrow corridor between Abbey Island and the headland above the beach. Note the cave-like apertures in the headland and the streaks of red-and-white rock that look like a Jackson Pollock painting. At low tide you'll even be able to walk to Abbey Island on an elegantly curving causeway of sand that's no more than a few inches higher than the sea around it.

If you round the headland opposite Abbey Island, you can walk north along the beach. There are no more sea stacks here but you'll have continuous views of Hoh Head and other coastal promontories. You'll also see a cluster of tiny offshore islets, including the pointed North Rock, on your left, and the wider, flat-topped Middle Rock, to the right of North Rock. On the shore to the right of Middle Rock is the lower Hoh River Valley (seen on Walk No. 28).

As you walk north, the piles of rocks and logs high on the beach to your right get taller and taller. The cliffs here are some of the highest on this part of the coast, reaching as much as 100 feet above the beach. Some of these gravelly bluffs have been eroded into sharp knife-edge spurs or ridges that run perpendicular to the beach. Others have been eroded into flat-topped, steep-sided mesas that would seem more at home in a desert than on a beach at the edge of a rain forest.

If you walk about 1.2 miles from Abbey Island, you'll enter the Hoh Indian Reservation. If you walk about 2.5 miles or so you'll come to the mouth of the Hoh River, where Indians often fish with nets. Walk as much or as little of this part of the beach as you like.

When you're ready, turn around and head back toward Abbey Island. If you want to avoid wet feet on your way back, return in plenty of time to cross the headland by the island at low tide.

Instead of following the trail back to your car, keep walking south. Almost immediately you'll see a cluster of handsome rocks in the surf just beyond the trailhead. If the tide is low, the mini-archipelago will be connected to the shore by a low, rock-studded peninsula of smooth wet sand. Attached to the rocks are lots of green sea anemones and purple and orange starfish sprawled in contorted shapes. Be careful not to step on or disturb them.

Keep walking south on the firm sand and, about .3 miles from Abbey Island, you'll come to a large, handsome headland. From its grassy top, water drips down its rock face and onto the beach, sometimes falling in steady streamlets, like miniature waterfalls. At the bottom of the headland are five picturesque caves. The largest, at the southern end of the point, is about 30 feet deep and 20 feet wide at the mouth. The others are all about 20 feet deep, 15 feet wide, and as high as your head. On the floor of the caves and along the base of the headland, a sheet of smooth wet sand is an elegantly simple paving.

Just beyond the caves is a striking 30-foot-deep niche on the south side of the point. Beyond the niche, the upper part of the beach is lined with long piles of stones topped with piles of bleached driftwood.

As you walk south, you'll get closer and closer to South Rock, which is only about .5 miles offshore, and the 3,000-foot-long Destruction Island—the largest island off the Olympic coast—which is about 3.5 miles from shore.

About .8 miles from Abbey Island you'll be almost opposite South Rock. Now you can see how this vertical-sided islet seems to be leaning to the right, rather like a slice of jellied cranberry sauce sagging to one side.

In another .2 miles or so you'll come to a low headland eroded into jagged peaks at its top; starfish are sprawled on the wave-washed rocks in front of it. Even at low tide, you can't walk around this promontory without getting your feet wet—which is why some people call it "Wet Feet Point" and why it's a good place to turn around and head back to your car.

Ruby Beach, by the way, is named for the garnet crystals in its sand, which sometimes give it a reddish cast.

30 Beach 6

This undemanding 1.3-mile round trip takes you along the base of intriguing dramatic cliffs and offers continuous views of Destruction Island and other coastal landmarks.

The Walk begins on Route 101, 5.6 miles north of Kalaloch Lodge. Look for the "Beach 6" sign on the west side of the road. An overlook on the bluff on the west side of the parking area provides a view of the beach, almost 80 feet below, and of Destruction Island, 3.5 miles away and almost directly offshore.

The 400-foot trail to the beach begins at the northern end of the parking area. At first the path climbs briefly through a pretty grove of birch-white alders; then it levels off and switches back and forth as it descends easily to the beach. En route you'll glimpse the ocean through the Sitka spruces.

Turn around when you reach the beach and look at the colorful layers of sediment in the almost vertical cliff beneath the overlook. Then check out the view to the sea. To the west, of course, is Destruction Island. To the north you can see several more landmarks: South Rock, less than 1.5 miles away; North Rock, to the right of South Rock and more than five miles distant; and the 200-foot-high cliffs of Hoh Head, to the right of North Rock and more than six miles away. About .5 miles up the beach is a jagged headland topped by two spruce trees.

For a close look at the headland, walk north. You'll soon pass a ravine cut into the cliff on your right. At the bottom of the ravine, a tiny creek trickles onto the beach and into the ocean.

As you approach the headland, the coastal cliffs become more dramatic. Some of them are flat-topped and steeply eroded on three sides; they look like mesas. Some have cone-shaped piles of eroded matter, known as talus, at their bases.

About .3 miles down the beach, you'll notice an interesting feature between the headland, which is perpendicular to the beach, and the cliff to the right, which is parallel to it. In the curve where the headland meets the cliff is a rust-colored depression that, from farther away, actually looks like a cave or tunnel that goes all the way through the cliff. Only when you're closer can you see that the tunnel is really a shallow grotto. The grotto is made of softer materials than the rock around it, so it's eroding faster. Someday the gnawing surf probably *will* carve a hole through the cliff and, after that, a full channel. When that happens the headland will be cut off from the shore and transformed into a high, wide sea stack. The last time we were here—a windy September day—we could actually hear small pieces of talus falling off the cliffs.

This point is directly below the Destruction Island viewpoint on Highway 101 and is the closest place on the coast to the island. Just 3.3 miles away, the long, low flat-topped isle looks a bit like an enormous submarine.

Except at low tide, you can't walk around this headland without getting your feet wet, so this is often a good place to turn around. On your return trip you'll have continuous views of Destruction Island.

When you get back to the path to the trailhead, keep walking around the tawny cliffs below the parking area and your vista will suddenly expand. Now you'll be able to see several miles down the coast to the south. Just beyond the cliffs is a large ravine with a creek in the bottom; near the mouth of the stream is a small pool filled with driftwood. The creek spreads out thin and wide across the sand before it enters the ocean, so you can cross it easily.

South of the ravine, the cliffs slope more gently than they do to the north, and they're covered with spruce and salal. The piles of rocks and driftwood below them, however, are higher than the piles to the north. You can explore this part of the coast on Walk No. 31 (Beach 4), so turn around here whenever you like and retrace your steps to the parking lot.

31 Beach 4

This undemanding 4.2-mile round trip takes you to the well-named Starfish Point, where you'll see colorful sea anemones, starfish, and other marine life on surf-soaked rocks. You'll also enjoy an impressive bird's-eye view of the coast, uninterrupted vistas of Destruction Island, and close looks at some interesting ship-shaped headlands and the fascinating holes made by piddock clams.

The Walk begins on Route 101, 3.3 miles north of Kalaloch Lodge. A 100-foot side trail on the ocean side of the parking area takes you to an overlook at the edge of a bluff almost 100 feet above the sea. (Note the burled spruce tree on your right at the beginning of the path.) Directly below the overlook is the beach, which, at low tide, curves gracefully seaward to meet the wave-washed rocks of Starfish Point. The gentle curve of the beach is elegantly

*Orange starfish and a seagull share the wave-washed rocks of Starfish Point on **Beach 4** (Walk No. 31), on the Kalaloch Coast. Destruction Island is on the horizon.* ▶

echoed by the parallel curves of the breaking waves, which resemble contour lines on a topographic map. This is a popular beach, especially among lovers of sea life, so you'll probably see at least a few people prowling about the rocks. Almost a mile up the beach to the south are the rocks of Browns Point. Destruction Island is 3.5 miles offshore.

After you've enjoyed the view, walk back to the parking lot. The trail to the beach will be a few yards to your right, at the southern end of the lot. The .1-mile path quickly goes down into a ravine, switches back to the right, and gently descends the north bank of the canyon. Then a wooden bridge takes you over some large rocks and a small creek at the bottom of the ravine. A sign on the bridge explains that the little round holes riddling these rocks were bored by piddock clams.

Follow the curving beach to the little group of large, smooth wave-washed rocks off Starfish Point. Clinging to these boulders are fascinating sea life, including sprawling dark-brown and orange starfish and clusters of blue-green sea anemones, whose shape changes with the tide. Walk carefully over these rocks, taking care not to harm the creatures that live here, and see what you can discover.

If the tide is low enough, keep walking around

◄ *Parallel waves break on the shallow sand of* **Beach 4** *(Walk No. 31) on the Kalaloch Coast. Starfish, sea anemones, and other marine life cling to the surf-soaked rocks at Starfish Point. Long, low Destruction Island is on the horizon, 3.5 miles offshore. On a clear day you can see its white lighthouse.*

Starfish Point and explore the beach to the north. The cliffs here are lower and less steep than those on other beaches in the area, and many are covered with Sitka spruce, salal, wildflowers, and grasses. Almost straight ahead of you are North and South rocks and the cliffs of Hoh Head. Nearly two miles ahead is the steep gravelly cliff above Beach 6 (Walk No. 30).

About .6 miles from Starfish Point you'll pass some interesting formations: a cluster of miniature headlands, none more than 12 feet high, that look like upside-down prows or sterns of small ships jutting toward the sea. Some of them are riddled with piddock clam holes.

Before you reach the cliff above Beach 6, you'll pass a total of four large ravines in the cliffs on your right—all deep V-shaped notches carved over centuries by the small creeks that flow along their bottoms toward the ocean. The last two creeks (including one near Beach 6) are often dammed into picturesque pools by sand and rocks piled up by the surf.

When you reach the trail to Beach 6, turn around and retrace your steps to your car. (You can explore the coast south of Beach 4 on Walk No. 32.)

32 Beach 3

This undemanding 1.6-mile round trip takes you to a rocky headland that's home to starfish, sea anemones, and other intertidal creatures.

You'll also have continuous views of North Rock, South Rock, and Hoh Head. As you walk down to the ocean you'll enjoy dramatic views of Destruction Island, the beach, and a creek at the bottom of a deep ravine.

The Walk begins on Route 101, about 2.7 miles south of Kalaloch Lodge. Fittingly, the sign for this little beach is smaller than those marking any other Kalaloch beach, and the only thing on it is the word "Beach" with a hiker logo below it. The number "3" is painted on a much smaller sign lower on the post.

The 400-foot path to the beach begins at the northern end of the small parking turnout and quickly switches back to the right. Suddenly you have a grand view of Destruction Island and a gull's-eye vista of the beach, more than 80 feet below. A sign here explains why the windward branches of spruces and alders on this bluff are truncated: "Strong, gritty breezes scar budding shoots, and salt spray invades the wounds, shearing back new growth."

The path switches back to the left, then back again to the right. Here, at the edge of a steep bank of a ravine, you have another view: the creek at the bottom of the ravine, 50 feet below, and the ocean to the right.

The trail switches back to the left again and traverses the steep bank of the creek as it descends to the

*The boardwalk curves around a big moss-coated western hemlock on the **Kalaloch Nature Trail** (Walk No. 33), on the Kalaloch Coast. In the rear are the twisting braches of a Sitka spruce. Salal grows in the foreground.* ▶

sea. At the edge of the beach you'll pass a house-sized boulder covered with spruces and ferns. Then you'll walk through a grassy swale and a pile of drift-wood high up on the beach, which is narrow even at low tide.

Turn left, cross the tiny creek, and you'll immediately come to a headland and a cluster of large, smooth rocks drenched by the surf. Here you can look for colorful starfish and sea anemones (take care not to disturb them). You'll also see rocks riddled with the tiny round holes made by piddock clams. (If you want to walk around the headland on sand, not rocks, you'll have to wait for a very low tide.)

When you're ready, turn around and head north, toward Beach 4 (Walk No. 31), which is less than .5 miles away. You'll see the cliffs above the beach and the signs on the bridge below them. You'll also have continuous views of Destruction Island, South and North rocks, and Hoh Head.

The sand en route to Beach 4 is smooth and virtually stoneless. The bluffs on your right are low, gently sloping, and covered with short, wind-sheared spruces, wildflowers, and grasses. When you get close to Beach 4, you'll pass small bare 6-to-12-foot-tall cliffs; the surf has exposed the thin, horizontal layers of sediment in their nearly vertical walls.

When you reach Beach 4 turn around and walk back to your car.

33 Kalaloch Nature Trail

This easy 1.5-mile stroll takes you through a remarkably lush, moist coastal woodland. You'll see a Sitka spruce with enormous burls, you'll have several views of Kalaloch Creek, and you'll see how a giant tree was harvested decades ago.

The Walk begins in Kalaloch Campground, on the west side of Route 101, less than .1 miles north of Kalaloch Lodge. To reach the trailhead, drive into the campground and take an immediate left (to Loops A, B, and C). In just a couple of hundred feet the road forks at a registration board in front of the rest rooms. Take a right, then an immediate left. (After you turn left, you'll see a sign on the right saying "Loop B.") In another couple of hundred feet you'll come to a four-way intersection. Take a left. The road goes straight, past another rest room building, and at a sharp left turn in the road runs almost directly into a two-car parking area in front of the trailhead. A sign to the right of the parking area says "Nature Trail"; campground sites A-52 and A-54 are close by.

A 50-foot path runs through the woods to Route 101. Cross the highway (while looking out for traffic) and follow the trail on the other side of the road.

You're now in a moist coastal forest of big old Sitka

spruces, western cedars, and western hemlocks with thickets of ferns, salal, and shiny-leafed evergreen huckleberry beneath them. Trees and logs are thick with mosses—sometimes so thick that they make the wood look green. So lush and prolific is this forest that its entire floor seems to be covered with large prostrate logs. In fact, it looks as if there are as many trees on the ground (albeit in various states of decay) as there are standing up—so many trees that the only bare ground in these woods is on the trail.

You'll walk barely 40 feet before you'll pass a huge stump on the right side of the path. Notice the two holes cut into the stump about four feet above the ground. When lumberjacks felled this tree, they stood on springboards that they inserted in these holes (a procedure described on page 132).

About .2 miles from the road, the trail splits into a loop. Take a left. Now you'll walk on a comfortable boardwalk. So wet is this forest that moss grows on the ends of the planks.

You'll barely start walking the loop before you come to an enormous dead hemlock, more than 11 feet thick. Notice the younger trees growing in it.

After winding clockwise for about half a mile, the trail approaches the north bank of Kalaloch Creek, on the left of the path. Since this bank is often flooded, there are no evergreen trees here, only moss-draped alders (often the first trees to grow in disturbed areas), as well as patches of grasses.

Then, on a wooden bridge, the trail crosses a tiny creek choked with a thick growth of sword ferns and moist logs covered with sorrel and mosses.

As the trail climbs up from the streamlet, you'll

see Kalaloch Creek, on your left, trickling over its stony bed.

A few feet ahead, on the right, is a large spruce with several huge, bulbous burls on its trunk; some of them are wider than the tree! (See page 209 for an explanation of burls.) There's a bench on the left side of the trail if you want to rest.

A bit farther ahead, side paths on the left take you quickly to more views of Kalaloch Creek.

Just a few feet beyond them, the main trail runs through a thick tunnel of tall salal, then returns to the start of the loop trail. From there you simply retrace your steps to your car.

To drive back to Route 101, take a right out of the parking area—the road here is one way—and bear right at the next two intersections.

34 Kalaloch Beach

This two-mile round trip is an effortless stroll along one of the smoothest, widest, flattest beaches in the park. You'll see Kalaloch Creek cutting through the sand and bare cliffs rising 50 feet above the ocean.

The Walk begins at Kalaloch Lodge. Follow the road past the housekeeping cabins, toward the ocean, and you'll quickly come to a break in the split-rail fence on top of the bluff above the sea. (There's a lightpole here and several Park Service signs.) Park your car and follow the 50-foot path down to the beach.

At the foot of the path, thread your way through the maze of logs washed up by storms, and you'll emerge on the broad, smooth sand beach. Just off shore you'll see foamy geysers leaping into the air as the surf crashes against the low, rounded Kalaloch Rocks.

Walk to your right and almost immediately you'll come to Kalaloch Creek, which cuts a crisp channel through the fine sand as it rushes past you to the ocean. Even in dry weather the creek is usually at least a foot deep and more than 20 feet wide.

After you've explored the creek, turn around and walk south along the beach. On your left you'll see steep cliffs, some almost 50 feet high, eroded by centuries of lashing tides. Some of the bluffs are too steep and too freshly cut to support many plants. Instead you'll see only long, naked layers of sediment, some tan, some golden amber; some stony, some smooth. Other cliffs, more gently sloped and covered with at least a little topsoil, support pearly everlasting and other wildflowers, as well as patches of evergreen shrubs such as salal, and stands of Sitka spruce, their branches pruned short by salt-laden winds.

The water here is so shallow that waves sometimes break far offshore. The beach is so flat that the shore sometimes seems like a vast prairie of sand on one side and water on the other—so flat that the sea coats the sand with long, wide layers of water that look thinner than even paper could possibly be. On gray, rainy days, the boundless sheets of water and sand seem to blend imperceptibly into each other.

About a mile south of Kalaloch Lodge you'll come to a deep V-shaped gully in the cliff. Like other ravines on this coast, this one has been carved by a small creek as it flowed into the sea. The Beach 2 Trail (Walk No. 35) comes down to the shore here, and the next section of the coast is part of that Walk.

When you're ready, turn around and walk back to the trailhead.

35 Beach 2

Like Kalaloch Beach (Walk No. 34), this is an easy two-mile round trip along a wide, smooth sandy strand. This Walk, however, takes you to signs of early lumbering.

The Walk begins on Route 101, one mile south of Kalaloch Lodge. You'll see a sign saying "Beach 2" and small parking areas on both sides of the road. You'll also see a deep ravine created by a small creek that runs into the ocean. The steep sides of the ravine frame a narrow view of both the beach and the sea beyond it.

The 200-foot path to the beach begins on the north side of the ravine. You'll barely start walking when you'll see, on your right, a Sitka spruce covered with about two dozen burls. (You'll see many more spruce burls, as well as a sign explaining them, on Walk No. 36, below.)

Walk another 50 feet and you'll see, on your right, a seven-foot-high stump with two horizontal holes cut into it about four feet off the ground. Before this forest became part of the national park, the giant tree that once grew here was cut for timber. Both the holes and the height of the stump are signs of "high stumping" (explained on page 132).

After passing more burled spruce trees, the path makes a quick, gentle descent to the beach. When you reach the shore, go left, cross the little creek and follow the beach southward. Like Kalaloch Beach (Walk No. 34), this one is smooth, wide, and flat, and the walking is easy.

As you walk south, you'll pass four deep V-shaped ravines in the cliff on your left; over centuries, they've been slowly carved out of the bluff by creeks flowing toward the sea.

You'll come to the fourth ravine about a mile from the trailhead. The beach to the south is part of Walk No. 36, which begins on the bluff above the gully. When you're ready, turn around here and head back to your car.

36 Beach 1

Besides a walk along a wide, smooth beach, this undemanding four-mile round trip also offers dramatic cliff-edge ocean vistas, an intriguing stroll through a fantastical spruce-burl forest, and a view of the mouth of the Queets River.

Beach 1 is narrow near the mouth of the Queets

River. If you want to explore it on smooth sand, not rough rocks, take this Walk at low tide.

The Walk begins on Route 101, 1.9 miles south of Kalaloch Lodge. You'll see a sign saying "Beach 1" and a long parking turnout on the west side of the highway. The trail begins between two brown posts near the southern end of the parking area.

About 50 feet from the parking area the trail forks. The left path goes directly to the beach; the right fork is the "Spruce Burl Trail," a .1-mile detour that curves through a grove of burl-covered spruces before rejoining the beach trail nearer the shore. A sign here explains that spruce burls—bulbous growths on the trunks—are the tree's response to "damage to a tip or bud." Scientists speculate that the damage could be caused by a "bud-worm-carried virus" or an "inorganic compound from salt spray," but no one really knows for sure. In any event, according to the sign, the intrusion causes "growth cells to divide more rapidly than normal to form these swellings."

The mostly level trail takes you through a surreal forest of fancifully shaped trees, some with burls that are actually wider than the trunk. Near the end of the loop, the trail runs close to the edge of the bluff above the ocean, and you can enjoy a dramatic bird's-eye view up and down the beach. You'll keep catching glimpses of the ocean as you follow the Spruce Burl Trail back to the beach trail.

When you reach the beach path, you'll be at the edge of the bluff again, and you'll have another dramatic vista. Directly below the trail junction is a deep ravine, eroded by a creek flowing into the sea, and a small wooden bridge spanning the streamlet. Clusters of driftwood are piled up just below the bluff; beyond the driftwood is the smooth beach, endlessly laminated by the surf with wide, thin layers of water.

The beach path switches back and forth down the steep walls of the ravine, past dark, lustrous sweeps of ivy, a plant that isn't native to the Olympics but somehow established itself here. After crossing the creek on the wooden bridge and walking through the tangle of driftwood, you reach the beach.

Like the shore to the north, the beach is a wide and almost level corridor of sand. To your left are sheer sandy cliffs topped by spruce trees.

Almost a mile to the south, you'll pass the South Beach Campground; you'll see recreational vehicles parked on the edge of the bluff above you. Here the beach gets narrower—if the tide is too high you'll have to walk on the stones higher up the beach.

The beach widens slightly after you pass the campground and enter the Queets Indian Reservation. There's no sign marking the boundary, but you'll start seeing handsome rustic-looking beach houses perched near the edge of the bluff.

About two miles from the trailhead, the bluff curves inland, behind the Queets River estuary; instead of cliffs, a large pile of rocks lines the beach on your left. As you draw closer to the mouth of the

*Huge bulbous burls on a Sitka spruce are silhouetted against **Beach 1** (Walk No. 36), on the Kalaloch Coast. The tree is part of a grove of fantastical burl-covered spruces.* ▶

Queets, the sandy part of the beach gets narrower—and the higher the tide, the sooner the narrowing occurs. Unless the tide is very low, you may have to walk on rocks again as you get closer to the Queets, and you'll probably have to climb over the rock walls to see the river on the other side.

After you explore the river, turn around and walk back to the trailhead. This time, however, follow the beach path, not the Spruce Burl Trail, back to your car, and observe the lovely open woods around you. The spruce forest floor is carpeted with a high but even ground cover of dark green salal and lustrous evergreen huckleberry. This handsome, gardenlike greenery is lower near the ocean than it is near the highway because, closer to the water, it's pruned by salt-laden winds coming off the sea. In the same way, salt air keeps the branches of spruce trees nearest the beach shorter than limbs farther away.

RAIN FORESTS

Walks No. 37-45 traverse the Hoh and Quinault rain forests, two of four temperate rain forests on the western flanks of the Olympic Mountains.

Hoh River Valley

Walks No. 37-40 all begin in the Hoh Rain Forest, in Olympic National Park.

To reach the trailheads, take Route 101 to the Hoh River Road, which is about 13.4 miles south of the center of Forks and about 22 miles north of Kalaloch Lodge.

After following the paved two-lane road for about four miles, you'll start having occasional views of the Hoh on your right.

About 6.6 miles from Route 101 you'll pass a beautiful grove of large bigleaf maples. Their long, twisting branches, heavy with beards of moss, look like southern live oaks dripping with Spanish moss.

At about 9.2 miles you'll reach the **Hoh Springs Interpretive Trail,** on the right. Signs along the easy .2-mile trail describe the small dams, fish ladders, and other "enhancements" of the habitat of coho salmon built by Rayonier Timberlands and the state Department of Fish and Wildlife.

At about 12.3 miles you'll enter the national park, and about 3.5 miles after that you'll come to the **Big Spruce Trail** *(Walk No. 37),* on the right.

About 18.3 miles from Route 101 you'll pass the

small Taft Pond, on the left. In another .2 miles the road ends at the large paved parking area just beyond the **Hoh Rain Forest Visitor Center,** which has interesting exhibits about the rain forest. **The Hall of Mosses Trail** *(Walk No. 38)*, **Spruce Nature Trail** *(Walk No. 39)*, and the **Hoh River Trail** *(Walk No. 40)* all begin on the paved path just to the right of the visitor center entrance.

The only accommodation in this part of the park is a campground just south of the visitor center. There are several campgrounds outside the park, however, as well as a couple of small grocery stores and snack bars on or near the Hoh River Road. The closest motels, restaurants, and large grocery stores are in Forks.

37 Big Spruce Trail

This quick and easy .1-mile loop—one of the shortest Great Walks in the park—is a delightful stroll to the banks of the Hoh, through one of the loveliest stretches of rain forest in the Olympics. You'll see four giant evergreen trees and at least a half-dozen other very large specimens; bigleaf maple trees with luxurious coatings of moss; and beautiful solid, gardenlike sweeps of sorrel and sword ferns.

The Walk begins at a giant Sitka spruce on the south side of the Hoh River Road, about 15.8 miles from Route 101. A sign in front of the tree proudly announces that it's one of the largest in the United States—270 feet tall and more than 12.5 feet thick at chest height—and between 500 and 550 years old.

Follow the gravel path to the right of the spruce and you'll quickly come to an immense red cedar on the right that's 6 feet across at chest height and 12 feet thick at ground level. On the opposite side of the trail is a large Sitka spruce, not as big as the one at the beginning of the trail, but impressive nonetheless.

After passing at least a half-dozen major trees, you'll come to another Sitka spruce, also 12 feet across at the base, on the bank of the Hoh. Note the long gravel bars in the river.

Now follow the path to the left of the spruce. After walking through wonderful solid sweeps of sorrel and ferns, you'll return to the parking area just to the left of yet another giant spruce, more than 12 feet thick at the bottom of its flaring, mossy roots.

38 Hall of Mosses Trail

This undemanding three-quarter-mile Walk through a lush rain forest takes you to the famous Hall of Mosses, a spacious grove of bigleaf maples almost completely covered with club mosses. The trail is also an informative introduction to the temperate rain forest; several signs describe the giant evergreens, "stilt

trees," nurse logs, and other woodland phenomena you see en route.

The Walk begins at the Hoh Rain Forest Visitor
Center, at the end of the Hoh River Road (described
on pages 213-214), 18.3 miles from Route 101.

At first the Walk follows a level paved path from
the visitor center. After a few hundred feet, take the
unpaved trail that leaves the paved trail on the left
and crosses the deep, placid Taft Creek. Then the
path turns right and parallels the creek as it gradually climbs up its steep northern bank. You'll pass
six-foot-thick evergreen trees on your left and large
dead trees sprawled across the creek on your right.

When you reach the top of the bank, the trail
turns left and immediately comes to a loop trail.
Take the left-hand path and follow the loop trail
clockwise through an ancient rain forest of giant
evergreen trees, bigleaf maples, and vine maples.
Moss is everywhere—hanging like long wispy goat-
ees from branches, clinging to trunks, and enveloping rotting logs. Well-written signs explain, among
other things, how you can identify western hemlocks
by their "drooping tops," Douglas firs by their "thick,
deep furrowed bark," and Sitka spruce by "sharp
needles growing all around the branch."

You'll also pass many nurse logs. Signs point out
how these large dead trees, sprawled on the forest
floor, are so named because they provide minerals,
moisture, and growing space for rows, or colonnades, of young trees that sprout on top of them.
Slowly, the new trees send their roots around the
nurse log and into the soil below. When the log

eventually rots away, the roots of the trees that grew around it stand alone in mid-air and the trees look as if they're growing on stilts; hence their nick-name, "stilt trees."

About halfway around the loop trail you come to the celebrated grove of bigleaf maples known as the Hall of Mosses. Bigleaf maples seem to attract more club mosses than any other rain forest tree; they cover the trunks and hang like long green beards from the branches. In the Hall of Mosses every tree is a large bigleaf maple with many long, spreading branches. As a result, the grove is a vast, soft green outdoor room that seems to be filled with nothing but moss.

Near the end of the loop, the path runs dramatically along almost the entire length of a Sitka spruce that fell beside the trail. Almost 200 feet long and four to five feet thick, the giant tree flanks the path like a long wooden wall. A sign nearby explains that the average Sitka spruce grows five feet thick and 220 feet high in the rain forest and that some specimens are as tall as 300 feet.

When you reach the end of the loop trail, go left at the intersection and retrace your steps to the parking lot.

*A child, colorfully dressed for the weather, gazes up at a huge Douglas fir on the **Hall of Mosses Trail** (Walk No. 38), in the Hoh Rain Forest.* ▶